Bare Bottoms
and
Stinging Nettles

INTRODUCTION

This small area of north Warwickshire is steeped in history with castles, stately homes and a ruined monastery. Charity and 'dame' schools provided a basic education for a few children but by the time 'free education' became law in 1891, most villages had a church school.

Most village schools were not idyllic. Classrooms with few resources and no electric lighting could be dismal. Teachers struggled with unruly 'free-range' country children and, just like today, lived in fear of exam results and the school inspector. Cleanliness and school toilets were another issue and epidemics were commonplace of diphtheria, measles and chicken pox. Some children were kept away from school to help at home or work on the land whilst others were so poor, they could not attend, as they had no boots or shoes to wear.

Intertwined with the history are memories of past pupils and teachers. They illustrate, using their own words, what life was actually like. There are many happy and amusing stories, combined with childhood tragedies and poignant recollections. Also included are graphic and moving accounts of pupils who attended two 'experimental' schools 'hidden' in the countryside at Corley and Shawbury. Corley Open Air School was for sick, Coventry children whilst Shawbury Industrial School gave Birmingham boys who were destitute or had broken the law, an education and training for work.

Corley School May Day (1920's)

'Bare Bottoms & Stinging Nettles'
First edition. Published February 2005

Price: £13.50
(Available by post: £13.50 to include post and packaging)
Fillongley Publications
The Old Granary, Fillongley, Nr. Coventry, CV7 8PB
Web site: www.fillongley-history.co.uk
Email: susan.moore@o2.co.uk

ISBN 0 9515116 3 7

Whilst every effort has been made to ensure accuracy, no two people will recall the same event in the same way, so I make no apology for the fact that details may not be accurate and the author / publisher, cannot be held responsible for any errors that may have occurred.

(Photograph front cover: Astley School 1908)

CONTENTS

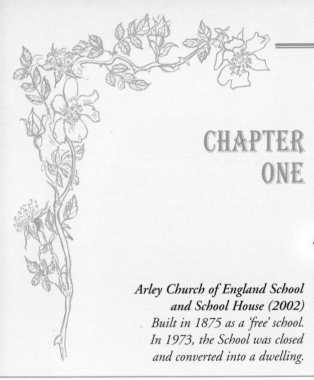

CHAPTER ONE

Arley Church of England School and School House (2002)
Built in 1875 as a 'free' school.
In 1973, the School was closed and converted into a dwelling.

ARLEY VILLAGE SCHOOLS

ARLEY CHURCH OF ENGLAND SCHOOL

The earliest school was in a room of a cottage that backed on to St. Wilfred's Church. William Avery had bequeathed property in 1732, to provide a basic education for ten poor boys in Arley and Fillongley and to clothe them in green suits. Extra contributions from the Parish and a donation from John and Frances Holmes, meant all children received a free education. The Church of England School was built in 1875 but the village was so small, that by 1897, the school was threatened with closure as there were so few children. The headmaster wrote in the School Log Book about his depression that the school may close. Little did he know then, that by 1908, there would be nearly two hundred children squeezed into the school.

In 1900, Arley was a quiet farming village with a small population of around two hundred. There was a shop, a post office and the 'Waggon Load of Lime' public house. Most of the ancient Forest of Arden had been cleared and scattered farms replaced the woodland. The market town of Nuneaton is about five miles away and Arley Railway Station, on the borders of Arley and Fillongley, opened in 1864.

At the turn of the twentieth century, Teddy Knox, a mining engineer, discovered coal and the first mineshaft was sunk in 1901-2. This attracted a steady flow of men from all over the country to seek work. Before long, some three thousand men, women and children flooded into the area.

Life must have been fraught for families trying to find somewhere to live in such a tiny village with no provision for housing, sanitation, schooling or other basic needs. We cannot begin to imagine how families must have struggled in the early days of the mine. As the mine prospered, new houses and amenities were built for the workers, but many families were large and poverty was accepted as normal.

In most villages, the Church Schools were under funded with little in the way of basic amenities. This school was badly let down by the School Managers. It was left in a desperate plight with ever increasing numbers of deprived children, some hungry and others had no footwear or adequate clothing. There were never enough desks and the school was badly overcrowded. The teachers did their best but in the early days, were badly trained. The school was extended but it remained a very small school stretched to its limits for many years. The School Inspectors reported on the situation but it seemed no one heeded the plight of the children or staff and pleas for help are found in poignant entries in the Log Books.

From the reminiscences of past pupils, we can see that many grew-up unaware of their poverty as they never travelled to nearby towns or villages to make comparisons with other more fortunate children. The stories these pages unfold, are a fascinating insight into the struggles, prejudices and successes of the children and teachers in the mining community of Arley.

EXTRACTS FROM
ARLEY CHURCH OF ENGLAND SCHOOL LOG BOOKS

1897 The attendance grew smaller and smaller and Mr. Avery, the headmaster became quite depressed with so few children in the school. Frederick Brooks - returned to the Workhouse. 9th November, Bobby Neil's brightness and activity of the previous week was like the last flicker of a candle. Saturday, he did not feel so well; Monday he passed away.

1899 The prize for regular attendance was given to Gertrude Thompson, the naughtiest and most idle girl in the school. Arthur Dexter, aged 5, was knocked down by a cow and trampled on.

1901 **Mrs. Edna Shepherd,** the new Head Mistress, discovered that dictation was learnt before the exam and made comment that exams were no test of children's work. 24 children on books. She taught arithmetic to infants by means of bead threading. A piano was given to the school by Rev. W. H. Poulton.

1902 The Police received a complaint that a boy named Alick Wheeler, interfered with children over a dispute between his brother and another boy. He came into the playground on his master's horse and used a whip and stick and on Friday a catapult. Police questioned him and he has promised not to do it again. Average attendance 33.2%.

1903 In June, the number of children attending school increased to 60 and the School Managers were informed that there was great difficulty as there were not enough desks. Mrs. Shepherds wage was £80. per annum. She notes that she would have to start using corporal punishment as some children had no moral sense. The boys' toilet was awful and she requested that it be put into a decent condition immediately. By November, 81 children on the books. The new desks arrived, broken! Some children away with with diphtheria.

1904 Many children away with ringworm and sores on their faces. Some away as they had no footwear and one girl had no frock! Children's feet suffered with broken chilblains. In March the school was closed due to an outbreak of smallpox among the colliery people. In April, the school caught fire. It began in the parlour chimney and the rafters of pitchpine burnt rapidly. They managed to save some furniture.

1905 The School was closed by the Sanitary Authority during May. Due to stress and over work, Mrs. Shepherd was having a problem to cope. She requested a new teacher to help but had to wait until October, when Matilda Reed, a supply teacher was sent. In the meantime, her husband helped her in the school.

1906 January. Mrs. Shepherd off sick due to overwork and her husband took temporary charge but had to close the school in February to look after his wife. 30th April, Edna Shepherd, resigned. October. **Mrs. S.A. Squire** became the new Head Teacher. 82 children on register.

1908 The problem of overcrowding was serious and 10 children refused education as no room. New classrooms were being built but by April the school numbers had increased to 187 and there were not enough teachers. In October, school rooms flooded again. Rev. T. Sampson - new Rector.
Inspectors Report - "Lack of interest. Inclination to talk. Staff inefficient. Condition of school - not satisfactory. Lessons too long. The infant teacher lacks experience."

1910 Frederic Orton, School Captain, left to begin work. Mrs. Squire ceases duties. April. **Mr. W. Jewsbury** – new Headmaster. Children were sent home for various reasons including - scabies, impetigo and verminous heads.
Diocesan Inspectors Report – "Religious instruction leaves much to be desired. Children are bright and intelligent but there is a lack of proper teaching."

1912 **Mr. C. Curtis** – new Headmaster. School closed due to mumps. Mr. G.H. Fowler talked to children about litter around the village. In October, a woodwork class began.

'Old Arley' The early village school was in a room of the
2nd cottage on the right. St. Wilfred's Church behind.

1913 - School Nurse gave a lecture on 'How to mind a baby' to older girls. Some children left to go to new Council School, 'Herbert Fowler.' 10 children returned, had gone without parents' consent.

1914 - Diphtheria. All books, plasticine etc. used by children with diphtheria had to be destroyed. 163 children in school. Children's footwear very bad.

1915 - Some girls were kept at home to help their mothers. Col. G.H. Fowler, (School Manager) was killed in action in Flanders. The Headmaster went to enlist but failed eyesight test - rejected as unfit. Walter Egginton and Frank Arnold, two old scholars, aged 16/17 enlisted.

1921 - Stanley Wallbanks removed from register – suffering 'auto intoxication'. In April the school changed to a Junior School. Mr. Curtis left to become Head at Herbert Fowler. **Mrs. Barnes**, new Head. In May, free meals given to all children of school age, due to the Miners Strike.

1922 - Mrs. Barnes resigned. **Florence Terry** – temporary Head. Mrs. Worton caused a disturbance as her children, Annie and Lily had been smacked by the Head Teacher. Marian Haine new Head.

1926 - *The School Inspectors Report* noted a big improvement in work and discipline. In May, children hungry due to the miners strike, and on the 20th day of the strike, the school organised free midday meals. **Marian Haine** resigned.

1932 - **Margaret May Joughlin** - new Headmistress. Electric lights installed.

1934 - Two boys passed entrance exam for Nuneaton Grammar School. 181 on school register.

1935 - All Roman Catholic children withdrawn and go by bus to Nuneaton. Milk supplied by the Co-op.

1936 - Rector held 15 minute service and spoke of the death of King George. Head Teacher in hospital. Five children re-admitted from Catholic School.

1937 - **Miss C. E. Pocock** - New Head Teacher.

1939 - Outbreak of War. The school was closed for several weeks and windows had paper pasted over them. 92 on register.

1941 - Miss Hutt from Spon Street, Coventry, came to help teach evacuee children. There were frequent Air Raid Alarms. Diphtheria immunizations were introduced in August.

1942 - **WAR YEARS** The war meant the school was very short staffed and Miss Pocock struggled with only one supply teacher from Nuneaton. 13th March, she wrote in the logbook:

"No enquiry is made as to how we are carrying on. No help sent. I notice that those who are so ready to criticise me, never enter the school to see how the work is going on, yet they still consider that they are in a position to judge. It would have been considerably more helpful had the said critics turned up to take charge of a class."

Weeks went by with no help. She wrote to Mrs. Hazel and the Rector to ask for help.

> "No one has visited the school nor have we received any help. Mrs. Tebbutt took whole school so that I could stock take. The Managers who should have done this have not concerned themselves. The far gate in playground is not kept locked and men are using lavatories and leaving them in disgusting state."

24th April, no coal/wood and it is cold in the house and school.

22nd May, Mrs. Pocock resigned. 2nd July – **N. Webb** took charge. 86 children on roll.

1949 - **9th May. Mr. Breeze** began teaching here today. School dinners began (50). Flat tables have replaced the desks.

SCHOOL CLOSED JULY 1973

The last entry in the Log Book was by Mr. Breeze, Head teacher.

> "There must be many, for one reason or another, will look back with affection on their time spent here. I am glad to be able to share that affection and must record my regret at the inevitable passing of the 'little' school."

Mr. Breeze became Head Teacher at Gun Hill First School. Mrs. Brook and Mrs. Turner retired. Mrs. Stockley to Gun Hill First School as Helper. Mrs. Martin and Mrs. Leake to Herbert Fowler School as Dinner Assistants. Mrs. Learoyd to Herbert Fowler School as cleaner. Mrs. Lincoln (caretaker) retired.

Log Book research by Mavis Hopkins.

Arley Church of England School (1960's)
Mr. Breeze, Headmaster, far right.(Back row) Mrs Stockley, John Davis, Tony Dawns, Theodore Selby, Julie Wainwright, Sarah Robinson, Diane Ward, Shaun Yewson, (?) Sharon Jones, Helen Reese, Darren Roberts, Tracey Whitehouse, Gregory Weaver, George Lakenby, Mark Newcombe, Carol Graham, Mrs. Turner. (Centre Row) Adrian Ward, Andrew Newcombe, James Graham, Sheena Osborne, Ian Brain, SharonYewson, Jane Thick, Julie Harris, Tracey Whitehouse, Karen Hawkins, Alan Howard, Andrew Brain, William Roberts, (?) Ian Ward, Heather Osborne, Juliet Hancock, (?) Karen Lancaster, Mrs. Brooks, Mr. Breeze. (Front Rows) ? Robinson, Jackie Brown, Linda Harding, Jose Knowles, Debbie Lackenby, Tracey Shore, Richard Yewson, (?) Lee Allen, Robert Downs, Diana Hawkins, Debbie Bindley, Kerry Harper, Ned Harper, Sarah Downes, Nigel Glover, Jill Osborne, Julie Buttons, Richard Ison.

Herbert Fowler Middle School (2003)

ARLEY VILLAGE SCHOOLS

ARLEY HERBERT FOWLER SCHOOL

Mr. Hartley had been a teacher at the Church of England School but on April Fools day, 1913, he arrived as Headmaster to open this new school. To his dismay, he discovered there was no furniture or water! The School opened a week later with 99 pupils. The headmaster notes – "The children are exceedingly backward and some of the more backward children are absent for weeks at a time." Some children were transferred from the over crowded C. of E. School and staff at both schools continued to cope with epidemics, overcrowding and severe social deprivation. The Mission Hut was used for several years as an overflow school until another school was built at Gun Hill in 1927.

During the early years, the school struggled and staff wages were reduced. Gradually, under the leadership of exceptional head masters, the school succeeded and became respected as a very good school.

EXTRACTS COMPILED FROM THE SCHOOL LOG BOOKS.

1914   Daisy Hill contracted Diphtheria. The two Cliff brothers had no food for two days and slept on bare floors. They were given cocoa and food by school prefects. Winnie Morris had two strokes of the cane for stealing from Miss Fisher's desk. Difficulty in finding accommodation for three lady teachers. **School Inspectors Report** – 'School not up to standard. Teachers are leaving to give their services for their country'

1916   Outbreak of Measles. Air raid drill. Huge snow drifts. Tom Spellman went to colliery – Mr. Knox saw his birth certificate, which showed signs of alteration and suspected he was not aged 13. Daisy Hill complained that the teacher struck her with chair leg. Daisy is a very disobedient, idle and backward child. Influenza epidemic. Girls aged 12 kept home to help with housework. The Lewis children climbed the school railings and took dinner bags. They said they could not come to school as they had no boots and had to wash floors. Mr. Goode has been killed at the pit. Subscriptions set up to buy Elsie Goode a jacket and hat.

1917   Concert raised £14. 18s 4d – sent cigarettes and oxo etc., to each Arley man serving 'the colours'. Joseph Spellman caned. Next day his mother complained – told Joseph to kick me if I caned him again and used insulting language in front of children. She has a grudge because eldest son, Tom, is not allowed to leave school. In one house, there are only three beds for twelve people.

1918	Whooping cough and Mumps outbreak. Fallen aeroplane – head took 4 boys to take charge. Influenza epidemic. Great difficulty in finding lodgings for teachers.
1921	Mr Hartley resigned as head master. The School changed to a 'Senior & Central School.' **Henry Curtis** moved from the C. of E. School to become the new headmaster. The school continued to struggle and suffer from lack of resources, overcrowding and epidemics.
1923	*School Inspector's Report. Mr. E.H. Carter. October 1923.*

SENIOR MIXED …Due to constant changes of staff and organisation from attempts to do more advanced work, when standards are not favourable, from closures for epidemics and that the school is in a difficult colliery area where home conditions are not so helpful, the school has suffered. Standard of work not satisfactory. Testing of work not thorough enough. Firmer discipline needed. School to be inspected again in one year." (After this report, the school was deprived of its status as a 'central' school and no extra payments given to staff.)

(Mr. Carter, gave accurate and thoughtful reports about the various schools he visited. He lived at Arley House, Fillongley and was very interested in local history and wrote several books. He was killed shortly after his retirement in 1951. He got off a steam train at Arley Station on the wrong side, and was hit by an oncoming train.)

1926	MINERS STRIKE. Children were fed for ten weeks and boots and plimsolls were bought. (Money from 'Save The Children' fund.) To help overcrowding, a new school to be built at Gun Hill.
1930's	The School began to make reasonable progress and the 1930's also saw improvements in public health and children received free dental checks and eye tests.
1939 – 45	WAR. Male teachers left to join the armed forces leaving only three teachers for two hundred and fifty children. Retired staff returned and teachers were 'borrowed' from other schools. Fifty evacuees were sent to Arley. Children were encouraged to work on farms to help the war effort. In 1941, Arley gave £20,000.00 towards Arley War Weapons week, of which £630.00 was raised by the school (Mr Curtis retired in 1947 and is remembered with great respect. Under his headship the school made excellent progress and a name on the sporting field.)

School Name Changes: 1921 - Arley Senior and Central School. 1923 - Arley Council School. 1934 - Arley Herbert Fowler Council Senior Mixed School. (? Date) - Arley Herbert Fowler High School. 1972 – Changed to a middle school. Herbert Fowler Middle School.

Head Teachers: Mr. Hartley 1913 - 1921. Mr. Curtis 1921 – 1947. Mr. Williams 1947 – 1963 (died at school). Mr. Moore 1963 – 1975. Mr. Edwards 1975 – 1981. Mr. King 1982 – present day. *Researcher: Mavis Hopkins.*

(1945-6) Back row: Mr. Curtis, Ron Jakeman, Ralph Nicholson, Walter Ross, John Davis, John Bailey, Graham Whale, Mr. Reece. Front row: Tony Wyman, Les Rogers. (?) Joe Gilbert, Ron Finch?

9

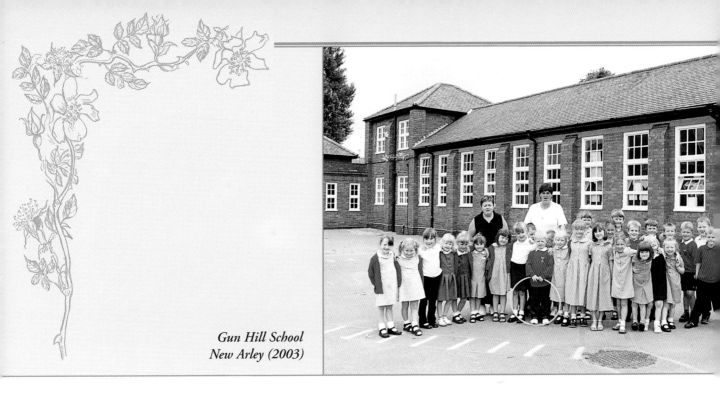

Gun Hill School
New Arley (2003)

ARLEY VILLAGE SCHOOLS

ARLEY GUN HILL SCHOOL

To relieve overcrowding at the Church of England School and Herbert Fowler, the Mission Hut at Hill Top was used as a temporary classroom. In 1927, Gun Hill Council School, New Arley, opened for one hundred children but almost immediately, the numbers exceeded this and doubled within three years. Like the other two Arley Schools, it was under-funded. Water pipes were defective, an open ditch and drains needed attention, insufficient lamps and not enough desks! The head teachers had many problems to cope with, including unruly behaviour and vandalism. In 1934, the School Managers received a deputation from the Parish Council, with allegations that the Head had exceeded her duties. She had punished three disobedient children who were found in the orchards. After lengthy discussions, the School Managers agreed that teachers had the right to punish children, even off school premises!

All schools closed frequently due to various epidemics and some children died of diphtheria. Inoculations became available in the 1930's and parents were given the option to pay for them. No child in the school received them, until they became free a few years later. It was generally accepted that most boys would follow in their father's footsteps and go down the pit. Sadly, many bright children were deprived of a better education and the opportunity to go to grammar school, as their parents objected. It took fifty years and two world wars to change attitudes. In 1947, two children passed the eleven-plus to go to the Grammar School in Nuneaton. This was a wonderful achievement and the school applied for grants and assistance from Avery's Charity, Miners Welfare and the British Legion. In 1949, forty-five children were eligible to sit the examination but only fourteen sat as parents refused consent. The reasons given were the expense of school uniform and books but there was also prejudice. 'Everyone should know his or her station in life!'

The introduction of school dinners proved a great success. The government introduced them nationwide, to improve the health of children and in 1947, up to two hundred dinners were served daily. The Nursery was full and most had breakfast, dinner and tea.

2003 - The school remains open and takes children up to the age of seven as a 'Nursery and First School' under the headship of Mrs. Saje.

The School Managers Books held at Warwick Record Office.

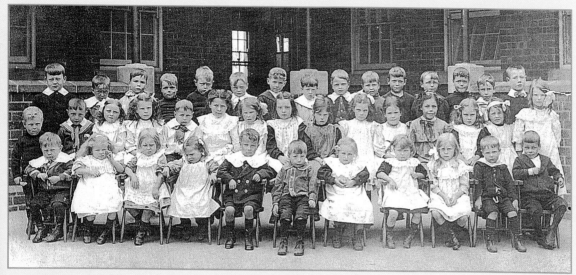

Arley Church of England School (1914c) Florence Markham, front row, 3rd from right.

Herbert Wright

I was born in 1904 and had had two younger brothers and one sister. We moved from Derby to Arley in 1915. It was a terrible cold November and we travelled on the train. We didn't have much furniture and we walked to our house up Gun Hill. They were building new houses and when they were ready, we moved into one. It was quite an event. They had the latest outside 'flush' toilets but no electricity. We were very poor with nothing to spare. My father had already had an army training before working down the mine and we hadn't been in Arley long before he joined the army. My mother got a pitiful allowance and it was very hard for her to manage while he was away in the war. She got a job working on ammunitions at Water Orton. I had to look after my younger brothers and sisters and queue for jam or lard at the Co-op and then be told off for being late at School, but Mr. Curtis was very understanding.

It was a very primitive track down the road that led to the Church of England School and the outside toilets smelled. Mr. Curtis was headmaster and he later became head at Herbert Fowler. The teachers were Miss Watts, Mrs. Garrett (became Mrs. Mathews) and Mrs Mason. We had prayers and a hymn each morning and Reg Tozer, who was a pupil, played the piano. We had religious instruction across at the church once a week. Our general education was poor, but sufficient for the times and the materials we had. If you passed the exams, you could have free entry into night school. I only had the stick once. We had to go every week for carpentry at Herbert Fowler with Mr. Palmer. One day there was so much snow, Mr. Palmer did not arrive, so we stayed and played snowballs. Mr. Curtis gave us all the stick for not returning to school.

I don't remember many childhood illnesses but I do remember the 1918 flu epidemic. Quite a few people died. Mr. and Mrs. Wherton died leaving their children. We were lucky that my dad returned safe from the war. He grew our vegetables and he would go for a walk with his little dog and return with a rabbit. We also kept a few rabbits but mother and I couldn't fancy eating one of our tame ones. We didn't have many clothes and shoes were a problem. If we hadn't got a good pair of boots, we were not allowed out. There were no shops. The butcher, baker, milkman and local farmers all came round. There was a boys club at the school with a miniature billiard table and we played cards and dominoes. If we were early, we could book the billiard table for 2d. When the older boys came in, we could sell this time and make a profit.

Rev. Sampson was a big, fine fellow who wore knickerbockers. I was in the Church choir. There was an old Harmonium that you peddled. When the new organ arrived, it needed an organ blower. I wasn't a Caruso, so it was one way to get me out of the choir. I got paid £4. a year for this job but I didn't see the money, my mother always collected it. I enjoyed school. We had no sports and had to put a penny apiece to buy a football. I left school when I was fourteen and went to the pit as an electrician. Mr. Staines sent me down on nights regularly when I was sixteen. There were fourteen ponies down the pit when I first started. Mr. Knox was a very modern manager and the mine was advanced with compressed air conveyers. I worked there for fifty years. The pit closed in 1968.

Compiled from oral recording (1999)

Edna Lucas (nee Parker)

My parents came from Stockingford. My dad got work at Arley Pit in 1923 and they moved into a new house in George Street on Christmas Eve. I was born in 1924. I had three older brothers and three younger sisters. We were a poor, but happy family. My dad was alright, not like some dads who were cruel to their children. He cultivated our back garden and had an allotment. Mother had a big stew pot with all sorts of things in it, sometimes rabbits. Meat usually went to my dad and brothers. It was thought they needed it more than us girls.

Our clothes were not very good. If we had one to wash and one to wear, we were lucky. We rarely had fruit. The 'Banana Queen' came round on a Sunday morning. She had a stall on Nuneaton market and sold off what was left over. She would call out, "Eight a bob bananas." Now and again, as a treat, we had a banana, sometimes with custard and lots of bread and butter.

GUN HILL SCHOOL

I went to Gun Hill School when it opened in 1927. We had storybooks and there was a library in the Welfare Hall in Ransom Road. There were lots of children, often forty in a class. My brothers went to the school in the Mission Hut until Gun Hill School opened. Every so often, a government person looked at our shoes. If we were lucky, we had a new pair of boots. They were heavy and high up above the ankles, with hooks and laces. I had an accident and broke my wrist when I fell off a slide in the recreation ground. I was in hospital for a month. When I went back to school, I didn't know my sums. All of us who couldn't do them had to go up and be caned. I was caned on my broken wrist and my mother went to school and told the teacher off.

MR. CURTIS

I went to Herbert Fowler when I was eleven. The classes were graded A, B and C. Mr. Curtis was headmaster and he wanted my brothers to sit the entrance exam for grammar school. My mum wouldn't let them, as they couldn't afford to pay for the uniform or the books. When Edward VIII abdicated, I remember Mr. Curtis telling us about it in assembly. He wrapped his watch chain round and round his fingers while he told us and tears were running down his cheeks.

Herbert Fowler (2003)

FLEAS & HEADLICE

Everyone got head lice, as they do nowadays. We had 'Derbac Soap' to wash our hair in. It smelt horrible! My mother had a toothcomb and combed our hair over paper. The fleas and head lice would drop onto the paper and my mother would squash them! My mother would put powder round the bed frame as a precaution against 'bugs.' They came and fumigated our bedroom when Doris caught diphtheria. She was in the isolation hospital a long time. If there was a bad accident at the pit, the buzzer went. Everyone would rush towards the pit gates. Mr. Dingley and Mr. Hawksworth both died and they lived in our road.

We rarely went out of the village so it was a big thing, the 'Poor Children's Outing.' Just about every child in the village went, as we were all poor children. Our favourite place was Wicksteed Park. The busses lined up at Gun Hill and we had a coloured badge to find our way back to the right bus. We had a really good time and lovely meal. St. Michael's Church opened about the same time as Gun Hill School. I have many happy memories. On Anniversary Sunday, we paraded round the village with the Arley Band. We had a new dress and a straw hat with little flowers and ribbon. Every Sunday, we attended Morning Service and then Sunday school in the afternoon and when we were older, Evensong as well.

Compiled from oral recording (1999)

Reg Rowley

In 1929, my father (George Rowley) obtained a job at Arley Colliery. My father put all our worldly goods on a cart drawn by an aged horse and it trudged the few miles from Ansley Common. We acquired a brand new house, 59 Charles Street, Gun Hill, New Arley.

There was no electricity and we had little furniture. We were then three children and my sister, brother and myself, all slept in the same bed. Later Mother had two more children. During our six-year stay at Charles Street, I remember one luxury. We had a large army greatcoat on our bed, given by an army uncle.

Everything revolved around the colliery. They provided the houses, water, electricity and ambulances. You came to rely on the colliery for all your needs. Even shops were let to miners for their wives to run. Candles were the only affordable means of light. Later the pit generated electricity. The wonder of electric in those days compares to today's space probes. In the village, Mrs. Fowler was the Florence Nightingale of Gun Hill. People would call on her to help with any illness or childbirth before sending for the doctor, (who needed payment). Her family had come from the Black Country, and they had introduced the keeping of pigeons to the village.

My memories of home are of my drunken father ranting and raving and of my mother who tried her very best to send us to school, clean. She seemed to make us wash with carbolic soap on every conceivable occasion. Like a lot of other families, we were pestered with fleas. These were always blamed on the great many pigeon lofts that clustered the back gardens, so it was no disgrace when children carried flea marks. We had a bath once a week in father's tin bath.

Saturday nights we children would go to the 'Fir Tree' at around 9pm when our father would be in a happy mood. We got his attention by shouting at the door. If we were lucky, he would bring us a bag of crisps. Although he would have enjoyed himself with his mates, he would curse and rant at mother. We were in bed and kept very quiet in case he gave us a good hiding. We never understood the hard life of a miner.

I attended Gun Hill First School for about a year and I can't remember much except that the school always seemed cold and smelt of lamp oil. Next I went to Herbert Fowler at Old Arley. On entering class, prayers were said. We had double desks, often boy and girl together. Those who were more willing to learn seemed to sit at the front. Lessons included reading, geography, algebra, arithmetic, history, drawing, music, religion, sport and gardening. The school was very strict. If you broke a main rule in the classroom, the whole class was punished.

There were no school dinners so I had to run home to get bread and dripping or fried leftovers. Most of us, because of inadequate clothing, suffered from chilblains. It was usually mid morning before the radiators were warm. Teatime meal was often a bowl of stew made mostly from potatoes, swede and rabbit that our neighbour had poached. It was hard to watch the 'better off' children munching an apple or orange. We would beg for the orange peel or an apple core. Sometimes I would trade my school milk for a stick of liquorice or a gob stopper and occasionally I would do some homework in exchange for sweets.

Reg Rowley 1st left
Hilda Rowley 3rd left

Mr. Keen taught sports and geography. A 'cuff' around the ears was his idea of teaching, but he helped those who tried. Mr. Ealing taught science and general and threw small objects at pupils. Miss Downes was mild mannered and taught music, religion, reading and writing. Miss Pitman taught 3A, the top class. She was hard but fair and took an interest in our home lives. Mr. Curtis, the Headmaster, was feared by all and even the threat of being sent to him improved our behaviour. He often wandered around the classrooms, coming up with the most unusual questions to see if everyone was concentrating. He favoured the cane, but a few days afterwards he would make a point of having a fair interview regarding the punishment. He also concerned himself with social and home life problems. He selected children in most need of clothing and footwear for the 'Tribune's Poor Children's Shoe Fund.'

Miners did not have annual holiday pay, so to get to the seaside was a rare chance. Midland Red (bus) would take about forty children to such magical places as Sutton Park, Lickey Hills and Wicksteed Park. We would get sandwiches, cake and fruit on arrival. I cannot describe the delight in travelling such a long way. The Co-op Society party and Wesleyan Sunday School treat were grand affairs. Later in the year there was the chapel prize giving. 'The Bing Boys' raised money for poor children to have a Christmas party in the Welfare Hall and the food was never ending and such that we had never seen at home.

CARDBOARD INNER SOLES

Poverty was accepted. Our jackets and trousers were patched, invariably of different colours. Our jersey and shirts were sewn and sewn until even the merest effort broke the stitches. Footwear, after a while had cardboard inner soles and a boy wearing his granny's shoes was not a rarity. Although most fathers were miners earning similar money, the majority spent it on beer and cigarettes. We never understood why some children seemed better dressed than us.

Doctor's bills were unaffordable and we had home cures of mustard baths and goose grease. The Nit Nurse seemed forever at school inspecting our heads. Absenteeism from school was fairly rare because truant officer, Mr. Charley Clifford (he also acted as court bailiff) seemed to be everywhere on his bicycle. I left school in 1935. I got called to 'colours' at the outbreak of war in 1939. I was sent over to France and involved in Dunkirk in 1940. I was among many hundreds taken prisoner of war. I was more than pleased to receive a letter from my old headmaster, Mr. Curtis, while in captivity.

Compiled from memories written in 1988 by Reg Rowley.

Arley Church of England School (1920c) *Girl standing, 2nd left: Winifred Markham.*

Walter Osborne

ARLEY PIT

My father saw an advertisement for work at Arley Pit and came here about 1914. His family was from Higham on the Hill. He volunteered for the Great War, but they wouldn't have him because he was a miner. I was born in 1931, the youngest of three brothers and sisters. I had a younger sister and brother who both died. Our home was comfortable and we never went short of food, even if it was rabbit stew. Meat was expensive and father had his own allotment and was a good gardener. We also kept a few chickens and during the second war, two pigs. I caught the odd rabbit. I would wait until they went down the hole, some burrows only went down a couple of feet and you could reach in and catch a rabbit.

My dad was the best. He never hit us. Mother was a bit severe. He did like a drink at the weekend, mostly Saturday, with his friend Bill Chester. My father had an accident in the mine. There was a runaway truck full of coal and it slipped and ran over his leg. He was crippled from then on. What they offered him in compensation was so small he turned it down. He carried on working at the pit until he was seventy five.

SCARLET FEVER

Some families were very poor and we felt sorry for them. Big families were poorer. I remember children dying of scarlet fever and one lad, Green, a local farmer's son got a mastoid in his ear and he died. He was about ten years old and there was no penicillin then. We had head lice. Mother had a special comb. She combed the lice onto a newspaper and then killed them.

Miss Pocock was head of the Church School. I didn't like her. We had slates to write on and I don't think I learnt a lot. I was in the Boy Scouts and she was the Leader. I had never been far from the village and she took us on a week's camp to Stoneleigh. Charlie Harris, a farmer, took our tents and luggage and we all went on a bus. It was during the war and I remember seeing the barrage balloons over Coventry.

When I went to Herbert Fowler, Henry Curtis was the head. I was shy and didn't push myself forward. He tried to get me to go to Grammar School but I wasn't ambitious. I didn't tell my parents. I enjoyed football and sports but I wasn't interested in education except for English and History. Both boys and girls had to learn basic cookery. One meal was stuffed lambs hearts. I was so proud of it and took it home to mum and dad. Mother had a bit and then I had to eat the rest. Jack, my eldest brother, was twenty-one years older than me. He passed to go to the grammar school and then on to Leeds University. It cost my parents a lot of money and he was the only miner's son to go to grammar school or university in those days.

GAS MARK

I was at school during the war and there were only about four teachers. I had to carry a gas mask. The German planes came out towards Arley and then turned round to go back over Coventry. Local people thought they took a 'bearing' off Arley as the pit bank was lit up like Blackpool illuminations. Coal self-ignites and the waste coal was burning all the time. It's a natural phenomenon and they couldn't stop it. I was about twelve or thirteen and watching a film in the local Grand Cinema that we used to call the 'Bog Hut.' They stopped the film and Mr. Voce, the manager, got up on stage to say that Coventry was being bombed.

Compiled from oral recording (1999)

C. of E. School (1920c) *Head teacher: Mr Curtis. 6th boy standing, with bow tie: Herbert Jones, son of the blacksmith.*

Vera Osborne (nee Bacchus)

OUR CHILDHOOD WAS HARD

My parents came to live with my Aunt and Uncle at 5 Church Lane, Old Arley and my father who had been a farm worker, got a job at the pit. That would be in the 1920's. I was born in 1932, the youngest of four sisters. Our childhood was hard, but we never went short of anything. Mam and Aunt Sarah made all our dresses and we were all dressed the same. My Dad was put on short time at the pit depending how much coal was needed. He kept pigs and fowl, dug allotments and the garden, cobbled our shoes and to earn extra money, worked on a farm. He did vetting as well. He liked a beer but we were never short because of it. He had to give up smoking when I was born, as he couldn't afford it.

When I was eight, Mam had a rupture, which haemorrhaged, and she was taken to Queen Elizabeth Hospital. You were not told anything. You didn't know that a woman was pregnant until you saw her pushing a pram. You daren't ask questions. You had a clout round the head if you did and we never back answered her. Our Mam worked hard and was scrupulously clean. She was paid for dressing fowl and rabbits for people. We had to help at home. The pigs had to be fed, the upstairs Kelly lamps had to be trimmed and filled with paraffin, we chopped wood and saw to the fire and the chamber pots needed emptying. (The toilet was in the garden).

Our 12cwt of coal allowance was delivered by horse and dray and tipped on 'the backs.' It would not last and we would go and pick up coal that came off the pit lorries as they came round the corner. When we went for a walk, we always took a bag and brought wood back. The pits supplied electricity but to save money, we only used electric lights downstairs.

I started school when I was three. I took money to pay for my milk and my Mam gave me biscuits in a brown paper bag. There were about sixteen in the nursery. We had lessons and didn't play. We all knew the alphabet before we were four and we all knew how to write. We were told stories and had bean bags, hoops and skipping ropes for the yard. We were put into lines before we went into school and our shoes and hands inspected. The nurse, Miss Dilcock, came once a month and looked at our heads. A lot of kids had nits or lice and they were given a ticket to take home to their mum. We never had them. Scarlet fever, impetigo and diphtheria went through the school. Our first injections made us all feel sick and we had bad arms. There wasn't much diphtheria after the injections were given.

MISS POCKOCK

The teachers at school were Miss Pocock, Mrs Hands and Miss Watkins. Mrs Hands died of Cancer. She was a lovely storyteller. Mrs Payne was there for a while and then she had to go up to Herbert Fowler. Miss Pocock was the headmistress and she was very mannish, hair cut short like a man and spoke like a man. If two children started to fight, she would get a ring of children around them and they would have to fight it out within that ring. She was a humanitarian, hard but thorough – she didn't stand fools gladly.

We had a good education at the Church School. During the war, Miss Pocock was sometimes the only teacher. She had the little ones on one side and would set them work off the blackboard behind one door. Where the fire was in the middle, she would have another group with a blackboard. I was in the top group and our blackboard was by the main door. She'd be teaching one group English, another how to spell and another how to write. You never heard a word. She had a hard time but she managed it. She had to, there was no one else to help her!

Our Flo had just come out of hospital and Miss Pocock had told everyone to be quiet. Flo dropped her ruler and it made a noise so Miss Pocock wrapped her across the knuckles. Another time she had to go into the schoolhouse and she left one girl in front of the three classes and said to tell her who made a noise. When she came back and asked, the girl said we had all made a noise, so every child in the school had the cane.

Mrs. Hazel from Acorns Farm was a School Governor and when she walked in the school, she thought she was queen. She would find fault with anything. She thought we should go to church and not chapel. Miss Pocock thought that too, but she was a very fair person. Every Wednesday in Lent we had to go to Church whether you were Roman Catholic, Methodist or Church of England. Only Maggie Arness stuck it out not to go because she was Roman Catholic. Mother said we would all end up in the same place, whether we were Methodist or what, but we had to do what the teacher said. On May Day, we had a dance in the yard and on Empire Day, we raised the flag up the pole and had to salute it and sing 'God save the King'.

When I was about to sit the eleven plus exam, Miss Pocock came down to our yard and called my Dad all the names she could lay her tongue to because he wouldn't let me go to the High School. He told her he couldn't afford it and he told me not to try to pass. My Mam said I should try and she would go out to work. Dad said she couldn't because she was ill. I didn't pass the exam.

LOOKED DOWN ON

Miss Webb replaced Miss Pocock. She would smarm up to you if your father was a shopkeeper or a deputy at the pit but if your father was an ordinary mine worker, you were looked down on. I went to Herbert Fowler when I was eleven. It was a good school but the war was on and there were only three teachers, Miss Pitfield, Miss Poole and Mr. Curtis the Head. They fetched old lady Payne and old Mr. Williams to come back and teach. Then they had Mr. Steele who had been injured in the Marines. We learnt the basics as well as housewifery, sewing and knitting.

At the Church School, there were one or two boys that the teachers called 'dunces' and they had to stand in the corner. At Herbert Fowler, you were not allowed to be disruptive. If the children were a bit behind they had extra teaching at playtime. They were strict but fair. I left school at fourteen and stayed at home for six months to relieve Annie to look after Mam. I then went to a tailoring factory in Nuneaton.

Compiled from an oral recording (1999)

Herbert Fowler School (1947/8)
Mr. Henry Williams, Mr. Reece. Back row: Graham Bamford, Johnny Rae, Ken Clarke, Ken Orton, Graham Spencer, ? Cowley, Trevor ? Front row: ? Reynolds, Les Rodgers, (?), Ralph Nicholson, Tony Wyman.

Annie Parkes (nee Bacchus)

I was born in 1926 at 5 Church Lane, Old Arley, was brought up in no. 6 and I now live in no. 4. I started school when I was three or four. We had sticks to count with and a chalk board. In the afternoon, we had to lie on a rush mat but after a while you had a camp bed. Miss Windridge was my first teacher; she biked it from Water Orton. Children had to be seen and not heard, we dare not ask questions.

We were at the Church School until we were eleven and then went on to Herbert Fowler. The hall was divided by a blackboard on wheels to make two classrooms. The teachers would be one each side and it was moved back for prayers. There were about 30–35 children in each class. You could hear the other teacher which was a distraction but you had to get on. I wouldn't have liked to go to the High School – we were village people with village minds.

EPIDEMICS

Every time I came out of school there was an ambulance on 'the backs' taking someone away. Vera and Flo got Diphtheria and nearly died. They had to be taught to walk again. They were at Bramcote Hospital for a month or six weeks. They bought Flo a little two-wheel bike and I went mad about it because it wasn't fair.

Joyce had Scarlet Fever. They came and fumigated our house. We had to seal the bedrooms with thick brown paper and I slept with my Mam and Dad. There was a candle in the bedroom with sulphur burning and something else. I remember them taking our Joyce and Mary Mathie away, all wrapped in a red blanket, in the ambulance. Children died. I can remember the Chesters and Johnsons losing a child.

I was at school during the war but we got a good education. Mr. Curtis was the headmaster. There was Miss Poole, Miss Pitfield and Mr Douse. Although there was rationing, we did cookery, knitting and sewing. With sewing, you had to work your way up – knickers, a petticoat a night-dress and then a dress. The boys did gardening and woodwork. I left school when I was fourteen. The boys were expected to go

(1944) Joyce, Annie, Vera and Florrie Bacchus
(Dresses made out of bedspreads)

down the pit and join the 'Bevan Boys' but there were some very clever kids in this village. I thought we were a poor family, but looking back now, we were well off. You never heard bad language. There was a lady came to live in this village and she thought that miners abused their kids but they didn't. They loved their children. It was a good mining community and we all helped one another out.

Compiled from oral recording (1999)

Sheila Tozer

I was born 1934, at Rose Cottage, Wood End Lane, Fillongley. My mother was a tailoress, so she was able to make our clothes. I had four brothers and one sister. I would have had another brother but he died when he was six weeks old. Our cottage was two up and two down. It had no water but there was a pump outside, a soft water butt and a nice well by Broomfield Cottages. The outside toilets were at the back, through the coalhouse so it was a bit spooky at night.

Rose Cottage (1940) Mr Tozer, Bob, Mrs Tozer. *(Seated)* Shelia *and* Pat. *(Kneeling)* Roger *and* Alan.

FILLONGLEY SCHOOL DURING THE WAR

I went to Fillongley School and in the afternoons, we had to get raffia mats out of the cupboard and have a little rest. During the war, we went to school with our gas masks on our back. We used to look out for aeroplanes and if one flew over, we were told to lie flat on our stomach. They dug out trenches near the churchyard and we had to have trench drill. There was a gun called 'Big Bertha' at the army camp down Breach Oak Lane and when it went off, it used to make our cottage shake.

I walked with my sister Pat and other children to school. The teacher would ask, "Where's Pat?" Pat didn't like school and she would run home. My mum would hit her with her shoe. My mum did all the hitting, my dad never hit us but we knew we dare not defy him. Old Jack Whittaker was the headmaster of the senior school and everyone feared him.

HIT ACROSS THE FACE

We learnt to copy write, using a pen and ink on paper with five staves, like music. He would walk up the gangway to make sure you had blotted and if you forgot, he would rap your knuckles with a ruler. He hit me across the face for playing 'tig' in the classrooms and sending a blackboard and easel flying. My brother got the cane for giggling while we were learning 'Land of Hope and Glory.'

I stayed at Fillongley School until I was about twelve but my dad wanted me to go to Arley and have the same headmaster as he had. A couple of years later, everyone had to leave Fillongley School at eleven and go to a 'proper' senior school. Because we lived more than two miles away, I was given a 'school bike' by the education authority.

HERBERT FOWLER WAS A LOT BIGGER

Herbert Fowler was a lot bigger and we kept changing classrooms for different lessons, whereas at Fillongley, we stayed in the same classroom with the same teacher. We had knitting, sewing, hygiene, history and other subjects. Mr. Curtis was the headmaster. I remember when he summoned everyone into the hall and we had to watch while he caned a lad for stealing a pair of pumps. It was a bendy cane and the boy cried. Mr. Henry Williams was the next headmaster and he was a bit softer. The school was divided up into four houses, Woolf, Cooke, Clive and Rhodes. I was captain of Woolf and our house won the cup. It was presented by Mrs. Hazel, whom we thought of as a 'big wig'.

My first holiday was a week in London with the school. We stayed in a Youth Hostel at Highgate. It was very exciting and we visited Buckingham Palace, the Houses of Parliament and many other places. I liked school and ended up as head girl. I left when I was fifteen to help my aunt and uncle on Acorn farm. Later I became a driver on the school bus service.

Compiled from oral recording in (1999)

CHAPTER TWO

Astley School (1908)

ASTLEY SCHOOL

THE VILLAGE SCHOOL

The school and schoolhouse are sited close to the Church and Astley Castle. The school was very small and as with most 'church' schools, had few resources. The first records of a village school go back to 1806 when Frances Newdegate supported a school. This may have been held in a room of the schoolhouse where the mistress lived. In 1871, a 'new' school was built next to the schoolhouse, by the Newdegate's. It was designed to take up to one hundred children, although fifty were the average. It would be difficult to imagine today, how so many could have fitted into a schoolroom 31ft by 18ft and a classroom 15ft by 9ft.

After the Free Education Act of 1891, the school became maintained as a Church School and little money was spent on maintenance or facilities. It was, however, a happy school and children grew up as individuals with a sense of belonging to a community and an understanding of Astley's important history. In 1926 there were 37 children on the roll. 1968 – 36. 1973 – 17. In 1970, the head teacher, Mrs. Halls died and numbers declined with the threat of school closure. The school was closed in 1973.

HISTORIC ASTLEY

In 1841, Astley had 371 inhabitants, 64 houses, one blacksmith and one beerhouse. In the fourteenth century, Thomas de Astley replaced the Saxon Church with a beautiful collegiate church which resembled a small cathedral. The tall church tower was covered in lead and was so conspicuous, it was known as the 'lantern of Arden' and at night it was lit to guide travellers through the forest. From the time of King John, the Manor of Astley was owned by the de Astley family and then passed by marriage to the Grey family. Sir John Grey was killed in 1461, during the Wars of the Roses. His widow, Elizabeth Woodville, appealed to King Edward IV to return some land for her two sons. He was so captivated by her beauty, they were married. Their daughter, Princess Elizabeth, married Henry VII.

In 1553, after the death of Edward VI, Henry Grey, Duke of Suffolk, attempted to make his young daughter, Lady Jane Grey, Queen of England. Eight days later, Mary, the daughter of Henry VIII, was also proclaimed Queen. Lady Jane and her husband were executed but her father was pardoned until he later campaigned against the marriage of Mary to Phillip of Spain. He hid for several days in a large hollow oak tree near Astley Church until he was betrayed by his keeper and taken to London where he was beheaded. The Church today is smaller than the original as the tower was stripped of lead and collapsed on the church in 1600. It was rebuilt in 1607-8 by Sir Richard Chamberlayne as the imposing Church we see today.

EXTRACTS COMPILED FROM THE ASTLEY SCHOOL LOG BOOKS

The School Log Books, held at Warwick Record Office are a superb record of life in the school. They show how the head teachers tried to improve standards against the tight budget of the School Managers. The school was frequently closed and children died due to various epidemics. As early as 1889, it was thought that the state of the school toilets might be to blame! Below is a selection of extracts 1877 – 1926.

24th Sep	1877	The Rev. Potter informed us that Charles and Joseph Tedds and Catherine Hammons to pay 3d per week and all the rest of the farmer's children 6d per week to attend school.
12th Dec	1884	The late master, who was 75 years of age, appears to have been unable to conduct his school efficiently or even keep his Registers properly. The present mistress has only had charge of the school since the end of the harvest holiday and cannot be responsible for her pupil's shortcomings.
1st May	1888	Closed. Children had a May garland and went singing in the village.
26th July	1889	Mr. Evans came to look at drains and offices (toilets) and ordered new earth closets. 23 children sick during the last 9-10 days, thought from the drains.
19th June	1890	Gave a lesson in freehand drawing - found girls much more apt than boys.
1st Sept	1891	THE FREE EDUCATION ACT CAME INTO FORCE.
20th Oct	1893	Reported several children for irregular attendance. Excuse being that they had no shoes. Parents out of work owing to the 'strike' in the coal trade.
10th Jan	1895	Closed for 2 days. Many children with blister-pox, still prevailing since the summer. Five boys punished for snowballing during the dinner hour.
6th Mar	1896	Closed on recommendation of Sanitary Inspectors in order to prevent the spread of whooping cough. Two deaths have occurred in the parish.
17th Feb	1898	A death has occurred of one of the children very close to premises and on recommendation of the Doctor, the children have been dismissed. The case is membranous coup. Diphtheria - suspicion.
21st June	1898	A family of four, sick with Scarlet Fever. Many children kept away. Parents refuse to allow children to attend while danger of infection.
14th July	1898	Washing bowls, cans etc., placed in the boys and girls lobbies and this is a great convenience. Mrs. Downes appointed cleaner.
21st May	1900	Holiday to celebrate 'Relief of Mafeking'.
2nd June	1902	Half-day holiday proclamation of peace.
20th June	1902	A week's holiday, Coronation of King Edward VII. No celebrations taken place due to severe illness of H.M. Mrs. and Miss Clews of Astley Castle presented each child with a gilt bust of the King and Queen.
1st Oct	1902	The deferred coronation festival was held and the whole parish invited to dinner. Each child received a bun left over from the feast.
	1904	There are a large number of entries reporting a variety of serious illnesses infecting whole families, including scarlet fever, small pox, blister pox, mumps, and diphtheria.

ASTLEY CASTLE

The Newdegate family, owners of Arbury Hall, came into possession of the castle in the 18th century. Its castellated towers were dismantled in the time of Queen Mary. During the last war, the army took occupancy and since then it was run as a restaurant. Sadly, a fire in 1978 destroyed most of the building, probably beyond repair and the ruins can be seen from the side of the Church.

Astley Castle ruin.

EXTRACTS COMPILED FROM THE ASTLEY SCHOOL LOG BOOKS

24th Jan	1907	A little boy, Walter Orton was drowned in Astley Pool through venturing too far on ice.
26th June	1908	G. Sidwell collided with a horse and milk float. Badly bruised and taken home by Head.
4th June	1913	Cookery lesson in Schoolhouse.
21st Oct	1913	Arthur Rowley received a silver watch for perfect attendance for seven years and three months, only interrupted by an attack of Scarlet fever.
15th Mar	1914	Several away to see flying exhibition at Nuneaton. Mr. Hucks 'Looping the Loop'.
7th Sept	1914	Peace Bell tolled at 1pm. Children repeated prayer for soldiers and sailors.
10th Dec	1914	Girls dressing dolls and making fancy articles for sale in aid of Belgian Refugees fund.
10th Mar	1916	No coal. 28th March – deep snow.
18th May	1916	Several children ran away to see an aeroplane which had alighted in a neighbouring field.
30th Jan	1918	Teachers and children presented the Head Teacher (**Mrs. M.H. Shirley**) with a traveling case. Many other gifts were presented on her retirement after thirty years in the school.
4th Feb	1918	Entered my duties. **I.R. Tolerton.**
21st Feb	1918	Head drew attention of the Managers to the condition of the 'offices' (toilets). They are not sufficient for the requirements. Chairman: Mr. Heath, wrote at once to the agent.
26th Feb	1918	No action has been taken. The offices still in same condition as last Thursday and they remain so until Saturday when they are cleaned. The Headmistress herself pours disinfectant down each with little effect.
27th Feb	1918	The carpenter has orders to mend the seats. This however will not increase the accommodation, which is totally inadequate for the children and staff of the school.
22nd April	1918	Man looked at drains went away again. Pump broken. For the last week, Head has been making soup for the children's midday meal in order to save bread. About 25 take advantage.
6th May	1918	Nothing done to pump. Every drop of drinking water has to be brought from either the castle or castle gardens. As it is warm and fine, the infants working out of doors.
27th May	1918	Re-opened. Room decorated. Ventilation better now window opens. Pump and drain attended to. The offices have not been touched. The smell is most objectionable especially during hot weather.
20th Sept	1918	Half day holiday to pick blackberries. Over 40lbs picked.
11th Nov	1918	Eight children taken to Nuneaton to hear signing of Armistice proclaimed by town crier.
15th Nov	1918	School Doctor inspected offices (toilets). 7th March. H.M.I. called. Shown the offices.
24th Mar	1919	Board of Education - New regulations. The 'offices' were properly cleaned for the first time since the present Head has been here. They were done by caretaker's wife.
28th Apr	1919	During holiday, new offices began to be constructed. Only two. One boys' and one girls' latrine. No attempt has been made to do anything for the convenience of the teachers!
20th Nov	1919	Boys went to Fillongley to play football. They were badly beaten.
4th May	1926	General strike began.

Log Book Researchers: Mavis Hopkins & Dorothy Day.

Astley School (2002)
Closed in 1973
It became a sculptor's studio and is now Happy Days Nursery.

Lila Emily Roberts (nee Sayers)

I was born in Smorrell Lane, Bedworth in 1918. I have three brothers and a sister and we all went to Bedworth School but they were so strict and I had the cane a lot. I would be about eight or nine when I moved schools and went to Astley. There were two of us at first, then there were about six of us going from Smorrall Lane. I was the first to go to school on a bicycle and the others thought it was great.

Mrs. Mills was headmistress and she wasn't strict but she was a good teacher. It was like going from home to home. There were two other teachers, Mrs. Knowles and Miss Jacques. Every Friday morning we went to Church and the Vicar was always there. We went to Fillongley once a week to do cookery and the boys did woodwork. We used to go on bicycles and I had no brakes so I used to have to put my foot in the wheel to stop. Mrs. Mills used to send me to help Harriett do the cleaning and washing in the house. Harriett was a lovely little old lady, she was like a home help to Mrs. Mills. We were taught all about history, sums, reading and writing. Girls were taught knitting, sewing and embroidery and we also did dancing. Mrs. Mills played the piano. We had a morning service with prayers and everything. We never had many outings but we used to have Christmas parties.

The school toilets were outside and they were earth toilets and were always kept nice and clean. The heating was coal from the pit, which we had free from Newdegates. There were vents in the roof, which you pulled a cord to open and when it snowed in the winter, we used to throw the snowballs in. After dinner when we came in there were piles of snow on the floor. Even though it was very icy and snowy we didn't get sent home a lot and we never had much illness at the school. On May Day, we had a May Queen. All the children had to vote and one year all the boys picked me. I had a white dress.

My brothers and sister went on to Ash Green School and they were all better educated. I didn't do so well with my education as I could have done, if I had stayed at Bedworth where the teachers were stricter. Our minds weren't developed as much as they could have been. Most of the children were farmers' children. I was happy there and left school when I was fourteen.

Compiled from oral recording (1992)

Astley School (1928c)
Back row: Head – Mrs. Mills, Ken Marshall, Bill Allen, Wilfred Leedham, Harold Platt, Harry Sayer, Alfred Sayer, Alec Simmonds, Mrs. Kitty Turner holding Phillip Simmonds. Third Row: Charlie Leedham, Beryl Mills, Minnie Allen, Kathleen Warden, Norah Simmonds, Olive Neal, Rene Marshall, Lilah Sayers, Win Platt, Phyllis Horabin, Betty Wright, Harry Davis, Elsie Corley, Hilda Corley, - ? Bernard Robbins. Second Row: Ida Nash, Geoffrey Nash, Edgar Nicholls, - Nash, - Robbins, - Horabin, Jim Wind-. Front Row: George Sayer, Albert Sheaver, Charlie Wright, Ralph Forster, Norman Wright, John Robbins.

Rene Parkes *(nee Marshall)*

I was born in Nuneaton in 1919. My father was a miner and we moved from Keresley to Astley in 1928. We travelled in a horse and cart with all our belongings. When we came by Knowles Farm, Mrs. Knowles came out with a huge dish of rice pudding for us to eat. There were five of us children and we were poor but we had plenty of food. My brothers poached rabbits and the odd pheasant and my father grew vegetables. My brother, Ernie, was only two and a half pounds when he was born. The nurse told my mother that she shouldn't worry about him, as he wouldn't live. The nurse took clothes off my doll to dress him. My mother kept him in her bed, by her side, all the time. He did live and we called him 'Pip'.

BIG OPEN FIRE

The main classroom had an old fireplace with a big open fire and a guard round it. We used to sit around this fire and have our lessons when it was very cold. The vicar came in on a Friday morning for religious teaching, and on Wednesday the girls used to have to walk from Astley to Fillongley School for a cookery lesson. That's where I met my husband, Dewis (Spuggy) Parkes. He used to walk Lila Sayers home and Dennis Towers walked me home. It was years later that I met up with Spuggy and we got married.

Pip was ill quite often with everything that was going but the rest of us didn't get many illnesses. The nit nurse was Miss Dilcock. We put our heads down on the desk and she would go through your hair. If you had nits she would tap you on your shoulder and you went to the teacher to get a card to take to your parents. Everyone got the occasional fleabite. They were always a problem.

All sorts of people came by the school selling things. Each week a man came with fruit and vegetables and we called him the 'Pomegranate Man' as he used to sell them at one penny each. The ice-cream man used to cycle up with a sign, 'stop me and buy one'.

We lived just a few yards from the school in Church Row. When Mrs. Hoatson came to teach the infants, we had to leave, so she could live in our cottage. We moved to Park Lane Cottage, a little, old, two-bedroom cottage at Wood End on the border of Astley and Fillongley. I left school at fourteen and went into service. When I was eighteen, I worked for Jo Phillips at Oldbury Grange, the grandmother of Mark Phillips. I went into the army for four and a half years and returned to the Phillips' household. I met up with Spuggy again and we got married and lived with his mother at Wood End and then rented rooms at Astley Vicarage with Ivor Carr Gregg.

Our two sons went to Astley School. Phillip was born in 1949 and Christopher in 1954. They both had a good education. Like my parents, I started working at Astley School as caretaker and stayed for thirty years or so until the school closed. I saw many improvements.

SCHOOL CARETAKER

When we first went, the ink was made with powder and water and poured into the inkwells everyday. The seats and desks held two children with tip-up seats. They were very heavy to move with solid oak and iron framework. The floors had to be scrubbed every holiday. When they had new tables and chairs they were much easier to move. Water, toilets and a cloakroom with a washbasin were a big improvement. The children had not had a washbasin before.

They changed the open fire and put in a big coke stove that had to be stoked up at night and then raked out in the morning and stoked up again. There was no central heating or hot water but they did get a big electric fan heater to add to the heat. Mrs. Hall, the head-mistress, put all her energy into the school. When she became ill and died, the school ran down. A temporary head teacher, Mr. Jones, took over, but it was just a matter of time before they closed it. It was a happy school and I was sad to see it close.

Compiled from oral recording.

Kenneth Marshall

Ken Marshall, Pip Marshall, Ted ?
Arthur Roberts, the village blacksmith

I was born in 1921. My father, a miner at Keresley Pit, did all sorts of other jobs to supplement the family income. He was the vicar's warden and gravedigger. He worked on Percy Daulman's farm at Howe Green and emptied all the bucket toilets in Astley for both the school and villagers.

SCHOOL CARETAKERS

I used to help my father and when we emptied the toilets, we took it away and spread it on the farmers' fields. Both my parents were caretakers at the School. They worked hard and we didn't have much money. I went to the 'new' Keresley School when we lived at Keresley, but I didn't like it there. Astley School was much better. It was homely with a big fire. I was very happy there. In the summer, we had parties at Astley Castle put on by Mr. Povey Harper, manager of Griff Colliery. It was a big event and we had other parties and village celebrations at Astley Castle.

BARE BOTTOMS & STINGING NETTLES

In the winter, I used to follow the hounds and not go to school. I was punished by having lines to write out. The girls' toilets were wooden with buckets. The boys had a stone trough. The toilets did smell! They were horrible! We boys used to go behind the girls' toilets and open the doors and drag the buckets out when the girls were using them. Sometimes we poked stinging nettles and stung their bare bottoms. The girls used to scream and we got into trouble! I often got the cane. I was a sort of ringleader. The village pump was in the playground. I got my head put under that by Mr. Daulman for throwing snowballs at him when he was coming down the road on his bike. And we got into trouble for scrumping in the orchard.

I was fairly good at cricket and I played football for the school and scored two goals in my Wellington boots. I had nothing else to put on my feet! Once I had a pair of football boots that I soled and heeled. They had to do for going to school and playing football. We were all poor. I used to earn 6d a week by fetching the villagers' milk. I did other jobs and saved up to buy my own shoes. I left school when I was almost thirteen to work for Mr. Daulman on his farm.

Compiled from oral recording.

Astley Castle
(1950c)

Ernie Marshall *(known as 'Pip')*

I was born in 1931 and went to Astley School when I was four. I remember my first day. After lunch, Mrs. Hoatson tried to get me to sleep in a deck chair. All the new children had a deck chair, whereas the older children had a rush mat on the floor. I had never seen a deck chair and I wouldn't go in it. I also remember telling her that I didn't want to learn the A.B.C. as I could already read. She said I couldn't read. I replied I could read the newspaper, so she fetched the Daily Express from her house and asked me to read it. I amazed her because I could read it.

RULER ON THE KNUCKLES

We got into trouble for throwing bricks at the fence near the blacksmith's shop. We got the ruler on the knuckles for small misdemeanours and the cane on the hand for large ones. I broke a school window by shooting at a sparrow with a catapult and the stone ricocheted up and hit the window. I got away with that! I didn't admit it. I said the bird had flown into the window.

SKEGNESS SCHOOL TRIP

I'm not in the school photo of our day trip to Skegness. I was only little and wandered off with another boy, Gordon Nash. We got lost and couldn't find the rest of the party. I remembered my way back to the coach, so we climbed in and went to sleep on the back seat. Unknown to us, the police and most of Skegness was out looking for us but I don't remember being told off.

I got cattle ringworm when I was thirteen, it wasn't a problem, I think they treated it with iodine. Iodine and vaseline were the main things you were treated with. I caught nearly every illness including scarlet fever. Half of Wood End went to the isolation hospital with scarlet fever, but I stayed at home with a white sheet hung up at the door, which was disinfected.

I used to take the local farmer's horses to the blacksmiths in the morning. I would ride to school on the horse, leave it at the blacksmith for the day and ride back to the farms at night. Sometimes, two horses and I would lead one. You could hear the ring of the blacksmith's hammer all day at school. The blacksmith was my brother in law, Arthur Roberts. He was kept busy as most farmers had horses. There were not many tractors about. I got a good education at Astley. I came 2nd in the entrance exam for Coventry Junior Technical College and left Astley school when I was thirteen to go to college.

Astley School (1926)
(Left to right) Back row: Hilda Platt, (2nd ?), Beatrice Platt, (4th?), (5th?), Charlie Wright, John Nicholls. Centre row: (1st?), Hilda Corley?, Nora Simmonds. Seated: (1st ?), Harold Platt, Henry Hammond, Reg Gibson, John Robbins?.

Mollie Knight (nee Towers)

We moved to South Farm on the Arbury Estate in 1932. It was owned by Sir Francis Newdegate and is famous as the birthplace of Mary Ann Evans, the Victorian novelist who wrote under the pen name of George Eliot. We had visitors from all over the world coming to look and take photographs. My mother enjoyed this and read all of George Eliot's books. During the blitz on Coventry, we were asked to house George Eliot's piano and writing desk.

South Farm, birthplace of George Eliot (1999)
(photo by W. Podmore).

I was happy living at South Farm, a large sunny house with a huge garden but it must have been hard work for my Mother. There were four bedrooms at the front and two very large ones at the back. Downstairs, it had back kitchens, a huge pantry and a long veranda joining the backdoor of the farmhouse to the door of the back kitchen. There was an oak drawing room, dining room and sitting room. We had no electricity but we did have a bathroom with a flush lavatory, but in order to have a bath, my mother had to carry buckets of hot water upstairs! We played in a room known as 'the governess room' at the foot of the stairs. It was rather unsafe because the floor was rotting, perhaps because it was over the cellar, which was a dark, damp place, where we found the odd newt.

GAMEKEEPERS GIBBETT

Because of the distance, I didn't go to school until I was six. Mrs. Oatson was the Infants teacher. After the first day or two I walked the three miles home with the Robbins family and Dickie Griffiths. We often saw the gamekeepers in the park, Arthur Hammond and Reg Vernon. They had a gibbet

where they hung their stoats, magpies and other vermin, but this didn't worry us. When I was about seven, I got a bicycle. This was a great event! In the mornings, I went to school in the milk lorry, my bike with the milk churns. On my return home, I would share rides on my bicycle with the other children.

I really enjoyed school but needlework was my least favourite subject. I seemed to spend the whole of my infants school life knitting the dreaded 'baby's vest'. It started off pink and ended up sort of dead mouse colour and unwearable. My needlework was another disaster; my threads always knotted themselves up. We had nature study lessons, painting and drawing and I loved reading and writing. In arithmetic we spent time every day learning our 'times tables'. One thing that made an impression on me was scripture with the Rev. Ivor Carr-Gregg. I enjoyed the stories he told us of the Bible Lands. He had a beautiful voice. I knew from my elders that he had been with Howard Carter when the tomb of Tutenkamoun was being excavated and I had heard about the curse on those who disturbed the tomb!

BORING CLOTHES

The school had no toilets as such. We had an earth closet with a wooden seat. Mr. Marshall used to empty the buckets, he and Mrs. Marshall looked after the school, brought in the coal etc. We had no school dinners, and the playground was very rough and hard on our knees. In wet weather, the schoolyard was often under water so that we had to paddle through to reach the lavatories. We really did wear boring clothes. In the winter I wore a grey kilt with a bodice, a thick jumper and black woollen stockings which wrinkled round my ankles, held up, after a fashion, by suspenders attached to my liberty bodice, which both boys and girls wore as infants. My first 'pretty' dress was for the Coronation of George VI in 1937. The School had a party, all the little girls had to be English rosebuds, and my dress had red rosebuds on it and a frill around the bottom. I wore a wreath of artificial pink rose buds on my head.

One of the special treats was the school outing to Skegness. We all had to wear brown berets so that we could be identified. We girls tucked our skirts into our knickers to paddle in the sea, still wearing our beret of course.

Looking back, I realise how little it took to please us. Of course, no one had much then, but I know we were delighted by any simple treat. Our nearest shop was about three miles away in Stockingford. A small Italian man from Paladin's in Nuneaton came round with his fat little pony, with a big tub of ice cream in the little cart. If we had a halfpenny for a cornet, we were happy indeed.

Compiled from notes written by Mollie Knight.

Astley School Outing to Skegness (1937)

Anthony Proctor

I was born in Fillongley and started at Astley School when I was four in 1965. My parents would drop me off at school on their way to work in Nuneaton. Mrs. Tucker took the infants and I stayed in her class for about three years. Then I moved into the juniors and the bigger room with Mrs. Hall, the headmistress.

Mrs. Hall was taken ill and we had a number of supply teachers including Mrs. Ellis and a Miss Hyde. When Mr. Jones came, it was a bit of a shock to be taught by a man! He brought a lot of new ideas and different methods and I had a very good education. It was a happy school, we were like a family and it was a magical experience.

Parents campaigned to keep the school open and we were very excited when they thought they had won. Then we learnt it would close in two years. Some parents took their children away and numbers reduced as it was 'winding down.' The tragedy was that when the school closed in 1972, the village died. There was still a village blacksmith, Mr. Sutton, but no shop or post office. I passed to go to Bablake School in Coventry. Astley didn't prepare me for a school with eight hundred or more boys and I found it very hard to adjust. Eventually I made friends but I never enjoyed it as much as I did at Astley.

Astley School (1972c)
(Photo taken by Anthony Proctor).
Girls Skipping – (1st?), Susan Jones, Jeanette Sutton, Linda Winterburn, Debbie Winterburn, Leslie Fox.

Thomas Leslie Ward (1930c)
Known as Les, born 1921. His father,
Bill Ward, ran Corley Ash Farm and
his wife, Anne, made ice cream from
milk from their Ayreshire cows.

Les cycled all round the area on his
bike selling ice cream. His mother and
sisters, Betty and Ruby, also sold ices
from the farm gateway.

Compiled from notes by Anne Pargetter.

Corley School May Day (1920's)

(1910c)
Nellie Hancox with her children,
John, Tom, Arthur, Alfred, Dorothy
and Dennis. Rock Lane, Corley.

CHAPTER THREE

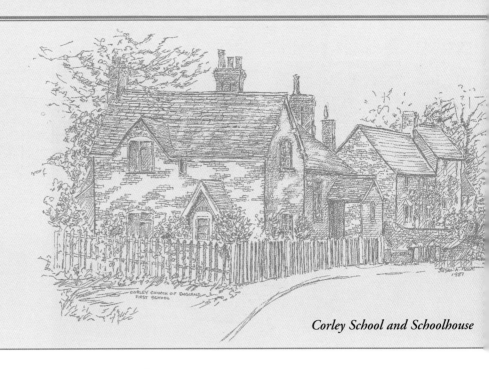

Corley School and Schoolhouse

CORLEY SCHOOL

Corley is a small, scattered parish that divides into three areas, Corley village with the church and school, Corley Ash and Corley Moor. Unlike other villages, Corley had no benefactor or charity to provide for poor children although a dame school was run at Corley Moor. In 1833, the National Society with local voluntary subscriptions, built a small school and schoolhouse on a narrow plot of land, next to the road. The children were to learn reading, writing, arithmetic and the Anglican catechism. The school, like most church schools, was under-funded and parents also had to contribute by paying a few pennies each week.

'THIS MOST NEGLECTED PLACE'

For nearly a century, the school was deprived of basic equipment, had awful sanitation, insufficient playground space and became overcrowded. 'Free-range' country children did not enjoy attending school and each new mistress describes the children's backwardness and lack of materials. To assist the mistress, a girl aged eleven upwards was employed to teach younger children and receive a salary of £10. per year. Teachers did not stay long and when the Managers dismissed one mistress because they discovered she had an illegitimate daughter, they could not find a replacement. Charlotte Bury agreed to come on a temporary basis and stayed for two and a half years. When she left she sent this letter to the School Managers.

> *Gentlemen,*   *12th October 1888*
> *After the unparalleled treatment I have received from you as my reward for nearly two and a half years, faithful, honest and hard work in this most neglected place, I can do no less than tender my resignation which I do with pleasure; merely adding that it was my full intention to have done so after the annual inspection.*
> *Marianne Charlotte Bury.*

From the School Log Books, we see improvements in the 1920's as a new head mistress, Miss Sutton, comes in like a breath of fresh air! Over time, the school was enlarged, playground space provided and eventually, the school blossomed and ended its days as a much-loved nursery and primary school.

In 1995, both Corley and Fillongley Schools were given notice that they were to close. A superb campaign was mounted as both communities united to save at least one school. The County Council agreed, but insisted the choice should be made by the Boards of Governors, chaired in Fillongley by Cllr. Ian Blythe and in Corley by Mrs. Evans. Fillongley was chosen as the better site and Mrs. Anne Pipe was appointed joint head of the two schools to steer through the amalgamation. The new combined school changed its name to 'Bournebrook' and considerable building took place creating a gymnasium, library, extra classrooms, kitchen and head teachers study. The school changed from infants, to an all through primary and junior school, with a nursery class in the old Sunday School. Corley School was closed in 1996, but not without a fight. The school and house were sold and are now converted into dwellings.

EXTRACTS FROM CORLEY SCHOOL LOG BOOK

13th April	1891	Commenced to teach drawing today although it seems a hopeless task without the proper apparatus. Cracked pump, no drinking water since December when the well was emptied for swilling the offices.
16th June	1891	**Miss J. H. Denman** commenced duties on a temporary charge. 'The children very nice and bright but unfortunately they talk too much. They lack interest and application at their work.'
1st July		Had occasion to complain of the boys using bad language. Gave a lesson on the sin and folly.
20th Sept	1893	I, **Marianne Charlotte Bury**, former teacher of this School, took temporary charge again. Some parents have removed children, others are sick. I find the school disorderly and rather backwards.
25th Sept	1893	Took a cane with me into school this morning. Find the sight of it has a salutary effect.
13th Oct	1893	37 in school. Some absent picking acorns and minding pigs!
20th Oct	1893	I have heard that the Managers have secured the cheaper services of a young person from Coventry. My work is therefore at an end. I had hoped to have pulled 1st, 2nd & 3rd standards through the ensuing Inspection. The 4th is nearly hopeless, but was improving in intelligence. Let the School remain in its dullness and disorder. Marianne Charlotte Bury. Oct. 23rd.
23rd Oct	1893	I, **Florence E. Hutt**, commenced duties as temporary teacher at the request of the Rev. R. Potter. Children very noisy and undisciplined. Received 2s 6d to purchase a few materials for needlework.
13th Dec	1893	Daisy Miller, monitress, absent this afternoon. She brought her dinner to school and after romping about and breaking one of the forms, went home with toothache.
8th Jan	1894	I, **Elizabeth A. Robertshaw**, commence duties with Edith Ashmore, aged 11 years as monitress.
9th Jan		Examined children and found them very talkative. Spelling and English very weak.
29th Jan	1898	I, **John Redfern**, Certificated Teacher, took charge of this school. The attainments of scholars were generally in a backward state. School suffering from a lack of suitable desks, stock and apparatus.
15th Mar	1898	Poor attendance on Friday afternoon, many children having gone to Coventry to see the circus.
25th Mar	1898	Cautioned the children against writing each others names in the offices (toilets).
1st April	1898	Very good attendance this week. Average 50. The present monitress, Edith Wale, received notice to leave, as I find that she is incapable of teaching or managing her class satisfactorily.
30th June	1898	Thomas Talbot, an infant, was seen playing with a half sovereign. He had stolen it out of the house where he is living. The Rector called on his adopted parents and he decided that the boy was to remain if he gave up thieving. If not, then he was to be sent to the Workhouse School at Meriden.
3rd Mar	1903	I, **Marie Elizabeth Mercer** entered duties today as Head Mistress. (Trained Certificated.) **Annie Frances Mercer** commenced today under Article 68, to take charge of the Infants.
25th Mar	1904	School to close as it has been notified that there is a case of small-pox in the neighbourhood.

Corley School (1906-7)
Front row: 2nd left: Hannah Elizabeth Falconbridge. 5th left: Florence Alexandria Falconbridge. 7th left: Alice Goodwin (cousin). The Falconbridge family lived at Lower Rock Farm and their father was a blacksmith on the Tamworth Road.

Below are names of some of the children attending the school in 1906, extracted from School Log Book entries 1901-6. (Many family names are still familiar today.) Lucy Allcock. Annie Arthurs. Lucy Anderton. Arthur Barton. Shaw Bates. Lizzie Courts. Ernest Courts. Evelyn Davies. Albert Victor David. Reginald Drane. Gwenderline Drien. Emily French. Ada Goode. Lizzie & Rose Goode. Nellie & Hilda Greves. Melvenia Harold. Daisy & Arthur Hutt. Albert Keen. Emma, Mary, Jane & Thomas Kimbrell. Roger, Archibald, Francis, Gilbert, Louther & Annie Knowles. Gwendoline Lowe. John, Donald, Ruth & George Mason. Florence Morton. Daisy Page. Ethel & Edith Pearson. Pollie Smith. Adela, Mary & William Smith. Yvonne & Thomas Stevenson. Amy, Gertrude & Sydney Stoney. George & May Steeley. Phyllis & Douglas Tandy. Harvey Thomas. Ada Ilkes. Frank, Alfred, Lizzie & James Winterburn. Mistress: Marie E. Mercer. Infants Supplementary: Annie Mercer. Monitor half-time (1905): Eveline Pearson.

21st Feb	1913	Only 35 children (42%) attended. Registers not marked but the children were kept in school. Three cases of Pleurisy, two cases of Pneumonia. (Stanley Warden died of Pneumonia on 22nd)
2nd June	1913	Mr. Carter H.M.I. called and examined the work. Owing to the backward state of the school and the lack of good grounding, recommend less time for handwork and more to the three R's. Infants Teacher, Miss Mercer, is recommended to go to a good Infants School for one month for training.
22nd Sept	1913	Admitted Chas, Ed, Albert and Joseph Hastings. Ethel Challis removed to Workhouse. 79 on roll.
30th Sept	1913	Miss Mercer, Infants Teacher, terminated duties today, after 11years. Children gave her a pendant.
21st Jan	1915	No coal in school for days. Very low temperature. Canon Fortiscue lent coal. Coal delivered 5pm.
11th May	1915	Admitted 2 Belgian Children. Marie and Andre Charles Lismonde. They speak French.
21st Oct	1915	Owing to shortage of labour on the farms, the boys are away from school potato picking.
17th Dec	1915	No fuel at all. Very cold. An airman came down with bi-plane - 26 children arrived late.
20th Dec	1915	School much too cold. Sanitary conveniences disgraceful, not emptied for a year. *A. Baker. Nurse.*
3rd Nov	1919	I commence my duties as Head mistress of Corley School today. Ursula H. Sutton A.C.P.
13th Feb	1920	The Teachers gave a Whist Drive and Dance. Profits £18. 17. 0d. We intend to spend this in beautifying the school by means of pictures and to improve the school sports by buying apparatus.
20th Feb	1920	We have commenced to plant the banks on the edge of the playground. I have divided the school into three divisions: - the Reds, the Blues, and the Pinks – House system.
7th May	1920	Mr. Marsh, Advisor of Physical Training, called. He considered the play-ground too small.
	1920	**REPORT BY H.M.I. Mr. E.H. Carter. (extract)**

"The present Mistress has made great improvements. The children have now learnt how to apply themselves quietly to their studies; their school life is altogether brighter, and the scope of their physical exercises has been happily enlarged by the practice of Folk-Dancing. There is still much to do. The future of the school depends upon securing more lively and efficient teaching in the infant's room. Both school-rooms are very crowded. The offices (toilets) need renovation..."

26th Feb	1926	24 cases of Measles. School closed. Sent 511 eggs to Coventry Hospital.
1st June	1926	Meals commenced for miner's children during the strike. 19 – 23 are being fed daily.
25th June	1926	Health Films at Foleshill Picture Palace – 16 children went on bicycles with Miss Tomlin.
19-20th Oct	1926	School Dentist – Mr. Harper – visited the school. 27 children attended for treatment.
22nd Oct	1926	Attendance low as children staying away the day following treatment by dentist. The Reading Room was used by dentist and paraffin stove used for boiling water and heating room.
9th May	1927	Cookery Class at Fillongley. 3 attended from Corley School.
30th July	1931	Closed school at noon. The old offices (toilets) were being pulled down.
5th Feb	1932	Rev. Dr. Frankland called to tell us that the Rev. Canon V.K. Fortescue had passed away.
29th Feb	1932	A fatal accident occurred on the road at 3.20pm. Doris Violet Gibson, aged 8, ran into a motor lorry, when she was looking back at Marjorie Lines, aged 11. There were no other children near.
22nd March	1932	Dr. Frankland and Mr. W. White visited school and heard repetition, saw written work and sewing. Dr. Frankland gave and presented prizes to: Leonard Lucas, Margery Lines, Dorothy Harris, Derrick Fletcher, Jack Steeley and Mary Lines. The head-teacher gave two prizes to infants: Joan Coles and James Henton. Mr. White gave nine sixpences to children who had worked well.
24th May	1932	Took Empire Talk, Union Jack and sang National Anthem. Closed for half day.

School Log Book & Managers Books at W.R.O. Edited version of Log Book 1888-1932 available from the author.

The last School Concert held in the playground by the school hut 1996, *a few days before the school was closed. Mrs. Sandra Leighton playing piano-organ. Mrs. Anne Pipe, headmistress, right hand side.*

Annie Rose (nee Gibson)

My father was born at Rock Cottage. He had three brothers and they all went to Corley School. He said there was just one classroom and forty-nine children. The little ones at the front and as you got older, you moved towards the back. I was born at Rock Cottage in 1917 but we moved to Staines Farm when I was five. I had five sisters and then my mother had my brother when I was ten. He was a poor little weazle. I used to mind him and I tipped him up on the muck heap one day! Staines Farm was a smallholding that belonged to the Warwickshire Coal Company. We kept some cows and did a milk round. There were paraffin lamps on the tables and we had a horse and cart.

I was five when I went to school, we had Miss Wilson and the headmistress was Miss Sutton. There were not many children and there was one big room with a screen between the two classes. There were two big fires and we used to toast our sandwiches at lunchtime, mostly bread and butter. I got a good education and got books for good work. We had no outings but we had Christmas parties and May Day was special. We used to do writing and painting for the Corley Ash Show. I don't remember having the cane but I did get a smack with the ruler sometimes.

TWO AWFUL TRAGEDIES

There were two awful tragedies in our family. I can remember my sister, Doris. She ran across the road in front of Corley School and was run down by a lorry when she was eight years old. As children, we had no serious illnesses except for measles. My sister Ellen Louise, died of measles. They went inwards instead of coming out. We called her Nellie and she was five years old. It had a bad effect on my mother losing two children. When I left school at fourteen, I stayed at home to help her. I used to take Jim to school; it was a lonely road from here. My elder sister, Mary, had stayed at home before me and she went to work at the Corley Open Air School as a House Parlour Maid and wore a uniform.

Compiled from oral recording (1996)

Corley May Day (1924c)
Left to right standing: Fred Gibson, (boy behind?), Doyle?, Gladys Betteridge, Ethel Weaver, Bill Smith, Girl?, Iris Gee, Boys behind Terry Harris and Eric Saunders, Boy at back?, Mary Gibson, Lily Harris, Boy at back Fred Foy, Boy in grey?, Annie Gibson. Behind - Bert Lyons, ? Stone, Charlie Page, Boy with flower stem -Paddy Meake, End boy? Front Row: Boy kneeling?, Grace Huckvale, Arthur Kenny, Nette Hodges, Mary Courts.

Bill Betteridge

My father came from Stratford upon Avon and went to work for Mr. Knowles at Corley Hall Farm. Then he worked for Bedworth Colliery stoking the boilers. It was a dirty job. He grew our vegetables and kept a couple of pigs for a hobby. I was born in 1923 at Highfield Cottages, Corley Ash. I'm the only one left of the whole family but I was supposed to die first. I had five brothers and two sisters. I was underweight, a very tiny baby and they didn't think I'd survive. I went to live with my aunt and uncle in Stratford upon Avon. They had only one child and could look after me better – I was spoilt. When I was six my auntie took ill and I had to come home. At first I was upset because I didn't know my own family. I was very shy and my brothers thought I was awkward because I couldn't talk properly.

We were a happy family but poor, very poor. The cottage had the water pump at the front and toilets at the back. My mother washed our clothes in a dolly tub and our clothes were all 'hand-me-downs'. Mum never complained. She cooked on an open fire in a big pot. Most nights we had vegetables and potatoes and we always caught rabbits. We had four ferrets. Mr. Hancox, our neighbour, was good to us and helped us out.

I started school when I was seven. I couldn't read or write and Miss Sutton hated me. She kept telling me I should be like my eldest brother Edward, he was clever, but that didn't help my confidence. I had days off, to see someone in Coventry to help with my speech. I was shy because I couldn't talk properly and it made me angry. I couldn't get my words out. I think Miss Sutton thought I could do better but I didn't like school and didn't try hard. The other teachers treated me pretty fair. The school had a big room divided with a screen making two classes. The infants' school was on the side. Then they built another room.

There were a lot of children and most were poor. Richer children went to school in Coventry. We played sports, football and cricket and I was fair at them. The 'nit' nurse came round. I used to get 'cow lice' and she couldn't tell the difference. You put your head against the cow when you milk her and you used to get them but they didn't live long on you. I had two ringworms off the cows. They itched and they started in a little spot, then got bigger and bigger and went round in circles. I had ointment to put on them.

When I was about twelve, after school, I used to work on the farm for Mr. Knowles. I fed the calves and collected the eggs. I left school when I was nearly fourteen to work on the farm. My father got coal dust on his lungs and when I was seventeen, he was in hospital and we knew he was dying. He asked me and my younger brother to look after my mother and that's why we stayed single. We stayed living in Highfield Cottages until 1994. Mother died about twenty years ago.

Compiled from oral recording (1999)

Dill Blount (nee Court)

I was born in 1925, at Highfield Cottages, Corley Ash, the youngest of eleven children. My mother had a small shop that she ran from the front room and my father had the newspaper round. He used to collect the papers from Arley Station. I went to Corley School and delivered papers on my way. Bert Kimbrell would deliver meat on the way to Corley School and Tom Kimbrell went to Ash Green where he would deliver meat to Ash Green School. We didn't have a good education, the teacher, Miss Sutton, believed in gardening, sewing and knitting. Nobody could spell who went to Corley School.

Compiled from oral recording 1985.
More memories in book 'I Remember Strawberries & Sewage.'

Corley School (1920c)

Frances James Gibson

A SIMPLE AND LIMITED EDUCATION

I was born at Staines Farm in 1927 and was five when I went to School. Miss Sutton, the headmistress, was all right. I remember breaking the window at school with a snowball; she told me off but we didn't have to pay. It was a simple and limited education but I suppose they taught us well. At the Christmas party, we were given an apple and orange. Old Tom Smith used to be Father Christmas. May Day was a big day with the maypole. I didn't get the cane, the teacher only had to look at you and if you did anything wrong, they would let your parents know. The vicar was old Canon Fortiscue and his butler used to bring him down to the school in a bath chair. Mrs. Basset Green was the 'lady' of Corley and she lived in Rock House. She visited the school sometimes. Her husband gave the Lady Godiva statue to Coventry.

I left Corley at twelve to go to the new Ash Green School. It was a long way and the Council paid five shillings a month towards having a bicycle. We did woodwork and metal work and had a gym. After school, I helped on the farm. For the last three months, when I should have been at school, I stayed at home and milked the cows and went on the milk round. You couldn't start before eight in the morning. There were no milk bottles and I knocked the doors to fill a jug, basin or jam jar. The milk was straight from the cow, not pasteurised. I got ten shilling a week pocket money until I married in 1951. I did the milk round for 46 years.

Compiled from oral recording (1996)

Joyce Buck *(nee Hancox)*

I was born at Highfield Cottages, Corley Ash, in 1929 in the same house as my father. My parents, John and Elsie Hancox, kept thousands of free-range hens in three fields behind the cottages. They also kept a couple of cows for our milk, a lot of pigs and dad grew his own vegetables so we always had the best food. The cottage had no electricity or water and the toilet was outside. At the front was one water pump to the four cottages. It was an unusual pump; you had to pour water down before you could pump water out.

I was the eldest of five brothers and two sisters. I helped to look after them and at weekends, I helped to clean out the chicken pens with my brothers. We were well off compared to other children and had anything we wanted and there were always little treats. In our row of four cottages, there were eight children in our family, seven or eight Betteridges, then there were the Winterburns and eight or nine Courts. Mrs. Court ran a little sweet shop from her front room. We all went to Corley School. We played in the fields and sometimes parents joined in, playing cricket and other games.

Miss Sutton was headmistress of Corley School. She was a biggish woman, well built with a quick temper and very strict. She didn't hit us with a cane or a ruler but threw the blackboard rubber at us. We used to duck, so she didn't hit us very often! We didn't have a good education, we had the bare essentials but I was happy there. We did a lot of games and sometimes went on nature walks through the bluebell woods. Every Friday morning we went to Church. Teachers were Miss Bacon and Miss Harrow. Miss Harrow took the infants and she was very nice.

I went to Fillongley School when I was eleven. The war was on and we had disturbed nights with bombers flying over, so after lunch we had a sleep under the desks. Fillongley was better than Corley. Mr. Whittaker, the headmaster, was very thin and tall. A proper 'sergeant major' type. He had a little office on the front and you could hear the cane coming down and the lad screaming. Mr. Darling was nice, a little man, plump and not so strict. Mrs. Spencer was there, she also taught my father.

Compiled from oral recording (1999)
More memories in Corley Open Air School chapter.

Archie Knowles

My grandparents moved from Kendal to Corley in 1900. They bought Corley Hall Farm in 1921 and sold it in 1948. They had nine children and my father was born in 1897. They all went to Corley School. There were about ninety children in one room. My father rented Corley Ash Farm from 1927 and I was born in 1931. I was five when I started school and I hated it. I wanted to be on the farm. One day, a salesman took me in his car to school and I refused to get out so he threatened to take me to Henley Market! I ran towards home and Mrs. Meek, who lived in a cottage nearby, tried to stop me. I shouted and called her 'fatty Meek'. Someone caught up with me on a bicycle and took me back. I must have been six or seven. In the evening I had to deliver milk to Mrs. Meek and she showed me scratches I had made on her hands.

The school was built lower than the field and seemed damp. The toilets used to stink! Our own toilet at home was a 'two-seater' up the garden. Miss Sutton, the Head Mistress was very strict. The 3 R's were most important to her. She was a typical 'old maid' and lived in the schoolhouse and had Miss Winterburn as her maid. She was quite artistic and liked drawing and painting. We had to do country dancing and I hated that. I enjoyed the nature rambles when we walked through Corley Woods. On May Day, our horses were decorated and brasses and harnesses were cleaned.

Miss Harrow, the Infant teacher, was very sound and kind. She was always smartly turned out. My mother also taught at Corley during the war. Miss Sutton encouraged the children to grow a garden down the banks at school and we grew flowers and vegetables. I walked to school most days but sometimes I took a pony and tied it up until lunchtime. I remember the war years. If the sirens went we had to troupe to a building at the back of the Rectory. We had evacuees living with us. We let two bedrooms and there was a family in each. The door was never locked so people came and went as they pleased. We had a gypsy caravan in the orchard and one family lived in that and another in the back of a lorry.

My mother encouraged my education and I passed to go to King Henry VIII's School. I had to catch a bus. There were queues of people each night to catch the bus to get out of Coventry. On the night of the Coventry Blitz, I remember people walking out of the city and a lot stayed in one of our old barns. How they survived in those conditions, I don't know. They had cardboard boxes tacked round the barn to try and keep the draughts out. We were lucky as children. We never went hungry and we were never short. It's something to be born in a house and still live in it. I've a lot to be grateful for.

Compiled from oral recording (2000)

Corley School, Queen's Coronation Party (1953)
Malcolm Gibson, Steve Huckvale, (?), Roger Cookes, John Shakespeare, (?), (?), William Barter, Leslie Watts, Stephanie Waugh, (?), (?), Margaret West, (?), Chris Barfield.

Doug Haywood

My father had been a miner at Keresley Pit. When he was 21, he had a mining accident and had his leg amputated. To make a living, he rented a small, one room shop called Highfield Stores at Corley Ash. At first, my parents had no money and their first table was made from a wooden orange box. Fortunately, they did quite well and I suppose we were better off than many. As my father only had one leg and he couldn't walk about easily, we had a donkey and cart, but the donkey was difficult to control and it would constantly escape from the fields. Then, my father had the only car in the village. I was born in 1933, one of five boys and I started at Corley Village School when I was five.

Doug Haywood, Basil Haywood, John Haywood, (?)

I have few memories of Corley School except that the teachers were strict. Mrs. Knowles was the worst; she used to hit your knuckles with a ruler. I remember the windows were very high up and all you could see was the sky. When I was seven, my parents sent me to Henry VIII School in Coventry. The war was on and I caught the bus with the factory workers. The Tamworth Road was much narrower, more like a lane with high banks. Most houses have been rebuilt or extended and the gardens changed from vegetable patches into ornamental drives and garages.

We had plenty to occupy us as we grew up. We enjoyed climbing trees, playing at Corley Rocks, going to the local farms, leading the horses and helping with hay making and harvesting. We rode the horse and carts, went fishing and bird nesting. Most children had egg collections. I went to the Youth Club held in the vicarage and we played snooker at 'Coopers' house. We played 'war games' with three teams of about twenty boys with wooden guns in the fields. The tennis club was behind the Post Office and I was in the first Corley and Fillongley football team. Corley Cricket Club moved to the rear of the Horse and Jockey. On Friday nights there was a film show at Fillongley Village Hall and Old Time dancing classes were also held in the village halls run by Mr. & Mrs. Joe Cheshire.

Compiled from notes and interview (Feb 2000)

Barbara Haywood (nee Marlow)

I was born 1932, in Foleshill, Coventry. My father had a coal round and he delivered coal all round the villages. When the war started, to escape the bombing in Coventry, he would collect my mother and me, and we would spend the night near Meriden. When father saw a cottage at Corley Moor for sale, he bought it and I started at Corley School when I was nine.

GIVEN A SCHOOL BICYCLE

Corley was a much smaller school than the one in Coventry. I was an only child and very quiet. I started in Mrs. Knowles class then went into Miss Sutton's class. Miss Sutton seemed old and passed her 'best.' Some of the children from large families were very poor. We did the normal things, maths, English, history and geography. I failed my eleven-plus and went on to school at Ash Green. I remember Ash Green being much larger and newer with good teachers, books, a library, sports and other activities. I lived more than three miles away so I was given a school bicycle to travel to school.

Compiled from interview (Feb 2000)

Mary Brown (nee Gavan)

We moved from London to Corley Moor in 1939, when I was three. It was the start of the war and we lived in a two up two down cottage called Ivy Dene. Upstairs was a tiny bathroom with a cold tap into the bath and we had bucket toilets up the garden. Lavatory men came round to empty them and we quickly closed the windows! Although we were a big family, we still had evacuees stay with us.

My first day at Corley School was fine. I was looking forward to a new adventure. The second day, I decided that was enough! It took my mother and Miss Harrow about ten minutes to wrench me off the taps in the cloakroom. I was screaming and shouting that I wanted to go home. I was five and it was such a shock leaving my mother, brothers and sisters. There were quite a few families walking and cycling together from Corley Moor and we played all the way to school. The worst thing about Corley School was that there was no window. It was strange being in four walls, like prison, after being free in the country. Break time was 'freedom.' Cold winds blasted across the playground in the winter and I would try to find shelter from the wind. Summer time – we liked to sit under the huge tree and talk about nature and dig round the tree and get out sweet tasting, whitish 'pig nuts.' When the Americans came through with the tanks, we were taken out to wave to them. 'Any gum chum?' We called out to them for some sweets.

When I was eight or nine, I was sent to the 'Christ the King' Catholic School in Coventry. I think my education started at this school. We had special lessons to help us catch up with our spelling, reading and writing. The school had windows and sports facilities. It was wonderful being there, compared to Corley. It was like being let out of a cage! We were probably the poorest family in the school and at one point we did have to wear clogs. Other children had nice dresses and shoes. We only had a nice dress for Sunday to go to Church. Mum made our clothes and she would salvage the material off clothes given to her.

We had a happy and loving childhood. Our parents were so good to us it didn't matter about being poor. My father worked hard but still had time to play with us. I had always got a little brother or sister coming along. I used to enjoy the new babies. It was something special. Everything was prepared and the front room was emulsioned and the family cot brought down. Mum had to stay in bed afterwards and Mrs Ellison and Mrs. Harris came in to help. The other girls in the village of my age had their little brothers and sisters to look after, but my mother wouldn't let us, as she wanted to do it.

Compiled from interview (2000)

Corley Youth Club (1952c)
Back row: Peter Courts,(?), Sid Courts, Bill Mather, Stanley Marriott, David Ward, George Dalton, Tony S…., John Wright, (?), Ron Barrick, Ernie Taberer, Keith Chadburn. 3rd Row: Mary Clark, Pat Chamberlan, (?), Bill Chadband, Eileen Taylor, Brian James, (?), (?), (?), Brian Taberer, (?), (?), Robert Farndon, Paddy Hancock. 2nd Row: Mr. Day, Eva Kimbrell, Rita Kimbrell, Pat Flinn - Youth Club Leader, Valerie Wills, Janet Mayell, Iris Reynolds, Eileen Taylor, Maureen Gavan, Brian James, Rosemary Reynolds, (?), Brian Taberer, Jerry Cooper, Michael Gavan, Paddy Hancock, John James, Arthur Cross. Front row: Rev.Gosling, (?), (?), Rose Warren, (?), Mary Warren, Mary Gavan with cup, Tony Clarke with shield, Marjorie Ball, Pat Green, Jacqueline Cook, Dorothy Smith, Janet Burns.

Clive Evrall

I was born in a cottage at Chapel Green, Fillongley in 1942. When I was four we moved to Windmill Farm, Corley, and I went to Corley School. I remember not liking school very much. I didn't like the teachers, the discipline or the boredom. The ways of learning, like threading beads on a shoelace or hours spent saying 'times-tables' by rote, was, as far as I was concerned, time wasted. My first teacher, Miss Harrow, taught me for two years. It wasn't a pleasant experience! She was rather an abrupt sort of person. I don't think she really liked children and she didn't like me. I learnt to read at an early age and spent a lot of time looking at books. I didn't like arithmetic and was no good at it. Miss Bennett taught me for a couple of months. She was altogether different and very kind. I was only about six and I remember her saying what a wonderful thing it was to read. My next teacher, Miss Harris, was severe and used a ruler to hit you. Sometimes she tried to make learning interesting, but mostly it was boring. Occasionally she read Winnie the Pooh and we had nature lessons, usually a bowl of newts or frogs.

Classrooms were cold in winter unless you were lucky enough to sit by the fire. At Christmas there seemed to be a truce between us and the teachers. They did try to make it a happy time with a magician and a mini feast in the classroom. We learnt crafts like weaving and 'papier-mache.' My last teacher at Corley was Miss Graham. I think she had a split personality. My reading was good but she didn't like my writing. My maths had not improved much from Miss Harrow's class and I just dreaded the lessons. I remember having to go out and stand in front of the class and do some sort of division sum. I couldn't get it right and she hit me seven times. If you misbehaved, she hit you with a stair rod. She didn't kill anyone, but she did slice one boy's arm open. My parent's never said anything about the beatings. They seemed to expect it.

I was encouraged to sit my eleven-plus and Miss Graham took a class of volunteers before school in the morning and taught them extra English. I left Corley School at the age of ten. I passed the exam and went to Nicholas Chamberlaine School in Bedworth. It was a good school and I was much happier there.

Compiled from oral recording (1994)

Carol Hawley *(nee Jarvis)*

My family moved from Wolverhampton to Corley in 1963. I was aged six when I started at Corley School. I think there were only two teachers, Miss Harris and Miss Graham was headmistress. Both were exceedingly strict and if you had to see Miss Graham, you would quake with fear. She was small and seemed rather old to us and she lived in the schoolhouse. We had to recite our 'times-tables' daily and had spelling tests regularly. I was good at these except when I had to spell the word 'surprise.' I had three attempts and could not get it right, so I received a rap on my knuckles with a ruler for my stupidity! On certain days we would have our elocution lessons. We had to bring a handkerchief to blow our noses before starting, so that we would be able to pronounce our vowel sounds correctly. If you forgot your hanky, you had another good rap on your knuckles. There were also enjoyable times, such as story time and nature walks when we walked, crocodile fashion, along the hedgerows and collected interesting things.

The toilets were in wooden sheds out the back. They were freezing cold in winter and many of us grazed our knees on the dark, slippery steps. The playground seemed vast and there was a massive Sycamore tree near the end. The girls played group games, 'a tisket a tasket' and skipping games. I achieved a reputation for writing the longest, most detailed and illustrated stories. Miss Harris organised a competition and the prize was a Maidenhair fern she had nurtured from a cutting. I wrote my story about an insect I had accidentally trodden on. It covered about 12 pages with illustrations. Imagine my dismay, when the plant was awarded to someone else, whose story was a measly two pages long. Miss Harris took me to one side and explained that although my story was the best, it was not up to my usual standard, whereas the child who had won had made a special effort and turned out his best work. This was a hard lesson! Miss Graham retired and Mr. Sherwin became Headmaster. He encouraged my story writing and changed the name of this class to record writing.

Compiled from notes written by Carol Hawley (2000)

Sue Bullen

I SAW AN ADVERTISEMENT FOR HEAD TEACHER

I was born in 1941 near Kenilworth. My father wanted me to study law but I wanted to teach. In 1975, I saw an advertisement for a teaching headship at Corley First School. Amazingly, I was offered the position and I started in January 1976, the same day as my daughter Kate, started school in Meriden. I was so happy. I had a fantastic job with wonderful people, in a perfect place with great kids. The best job in the world! The school had become run-down and parents were disenchanted. There were about twenty children, one teacher, Mrs Yeomans and myself. The nursery had only nine children and Mrs Whiteman was in charge. Almost anything I did was an improvement and the School Governors, Archie Knowles and Roger Cooper, were a great help. A lot more children started to come to the school and Mrs. Sandra Leighton was recommended to me as a teacher.

We split the school into two classes. I took the younger children and Mrs. Leighton took the older children. We were a very good team as we are so different. She is very organised whereas I'm not so organised, but maybe more imaginative. Her teaching skills were so sound. I had some teaching practice in a Montessori Nursery School where teaching is not ordered. The child can follow their own little routine and there were activities for learning. A sand tray could be made into a garden, fir cones would be imaginary trees and the children learnt how to count the trees in rows. This is a much harder way to teach. Our strength was that learning was child centred and not tied down to any particular method. We knew the children and parents well and we tried to accommodate them all and the children seemed to enjoy it.

SCHOOL TREBLED IN SIZE

The school trebled in size as the government relaxed rules, so children could come from outside their catchment areas. We now had three classes plus a nursery. Mrs. Pegg came in to take a class and we had another teacher, Janet Docker, for several years. Mrs. Spare came to help with the Nursery when Mrs. Whiteman retired. Jane Udall was a nursery nurse. Mrs. Mawby a school helper. (Pat Abbot a helper before). Nan – was a bit of a legend. We needed a dinner lady and Andrew Morgan called her Nan so all the children called her Nan – and she would stay and help anytime. Mrs. Mather was a health visitor and she was one of those people who also got 'roped' into the school.

Corley School (1976)
Back Row: George ? held by Mrs. Sue Bullen, Mrs Jean Yeomans, Mrs. Sandra Leighton, Mrs. Pat Abbott, Mrs. Jean Whiteman. 4th Row: Cheryl Bradford, Stewart Betteridge, Sarah Chambers, (?), Tanya Hancox, David White, Joan Lees, Helen Knowles, Gillian Harris, Joanne Hamilton, Conrad Miles, Andrew Ward. 3rd Row: Martin Heritage, Elizabeth Knowles, (?), David Hancox, Richard Lees, Richard Wall, (?), David Southall, Lorraine Harris, Maria Harris, Jason Chambers. 2nd Row: Neil Hancox, (?), (?), Claire Jones, Joanne Betteridge, David Aston, Steven Harrison or Michael Harris, ? Lynax, Emma Lovegrove. Front Row: (?), Rachael Pegg, (?), Alison Meek, Jason Lewis, Peter Knowles, Alison Knowles, (?), (?), (?), Andrew Harrison?, Martin? Harris.

There was so much going on and we organised trips, theatre and took part in celebrations, had Christmas plays and parties, sports days etc. The vicar, John Law, asked if I could start a Sunday school in the Church, which I did with Claire Morrisey. Blind children came in every week from Exhall Grange Special School and our children would go to Exhall Grange for a morning to see what it was like there. When the first Corley Show was organised, about 1986, the school was to be given the proceeds. When I said that we needed a computer, the school governors refused, saying that a computer was a waste of time and would never catch on! Rev. John Law was the peacemaker and eventually they agreed to buy one. When I left we had six computers.

In the early 1980's village Schools were being closed. We had already been up for closure once but with everyone's help, we fought a campaign and stayed open. We were victims of our own success. Schools were given their own budget and the administration became an enormous burden. I couldn't cope with teaching and doing all the paper work. After seventeen years of successfully running the school, my doctor recommended I retire. I was very stressed and had a heart problem. The job had changed so much. The National Curriculum was coming in. Term One – you will do this. Term Two – you will do this. I was cross and a bit bitter and I was very glad not to be there to see the school closing.

I believe that like plants and flowers – you let children grow at their own pace. You let them play and see the learning opportunities in play. We did the phonics and times tables, but only so long in a day. You can't make it hard work. They can do the hard graft later, when they are older. Trendies in teaching, don't understand, they have fashions and children have lost out by not learning to spell or read. What we do today, will affect life tomorrow.

Compiled from oral recording (2000)

Susan Moore (The Author's Memories)

We moved to Fillongley in 1980 and our daughter went to Herbert Fowler where she enjoyed the music and being a member of their wind band. In 1985, when our son Christopher was three, we decided to send him to the pre-school nursery at Corley. We were invited as 'prospective' parents, to visit the school and found the staff relaxed and very kind. The headmistress, Mrs. Bullen, seemed a little shy with new parents but happy to sit on the floor and play with the children!

TWO HEADED COW

We were delighted with the school and have many happy memories of the outings, May-days, sports days and especially the Christmas play. Christopher was the rear-end of the nativity cow but in the middle of the play, his head popped out making a two-headed cow! When asked why he had done this, he explained that he had to hold the girl in front but she kept making awful smells in his face, so he had to come up for air!

The staff were thoughtful and genuinely fond of the children and Christopher loved school and thrived academically. It seems very sad that small village schools are always targeted on cost cutting budgets. I was fortunate to be asked by the Vicar, John Law, if I would record the closing of the school by making a video film. The final days were mixed with both sadness and excitement as the new building took shape. I visited Bournebrook School after the opening and asked Corley children what they thought of their new school. Most said that they liked having more friends but that they preferred Corley, as it was smaller.

Christopher's Birthday Picnic (5th May 1989)
Johnathan Tatum, Sam Dyde, Dale Hirons, Joanna Gaine, Charlotte Venebles, Ashley Venebles, Nicola Wood, Mrs. Julie Venebles, Christopher Moore, Mathew Gaine, Rocky the dog.

41

CHAPTER FOUR

Corley Open Air School (1928)

CORLEY OPEN AIR SCHOOL

Corley Open School was a school conducted in the 'open air.' Children slept in dormitories with the sides open to the elements. In winter their only protection was tarpaulin blinds pulled down to keep rain and snow off their beds. Everything was done outside and children received a basic education and simple but nutritious diet. Corley became Coventry's answer to Switzerland! It is however, interesting to note the differences of opinion about how good or barbaric the school was, depending on whether you were an adult working at the school or a child attending against your wishes!

OPEN AIR CAMP

To understand why a special 'open air' camp school was thought to be good for children, you need to imagine what it was like to live in a city at the end of the 19th century. The population had increased dramatically and large families of between five and ten children were not uncommon. Poverty, poor housing, poor sanitation, lack of clean drinking water, smog and poor diet, all contributed to sickness and ill health. The social changes that were needed were enormous and improvements came very slowly.

In 1891, free compulsory primary education became law and this presented a problem for teachers and local authorities. All children were obliged to attend school but undernourished children could not concentrate and many children were too sick to go to school. In the early 20th century, with assistance from charitable organisations and philanthropists, more work was done to help sick and poor children, although the Work-House was still there for the destitute! In Coventry, a 'Children's Care Committee' was set up and cases of neglected children were reported to the N.S.P.C.C. By 1916, Coventry had 17,581 children who attended school, but another 2,269 who did not!

Some sick children were sent into the country to stay on farms at Fillongley, Hollyberry End and Corley. Most improved, although the lack of supervision and personal hygiene at some farms for the younger children, left something to be desired! Money was also raised to send children to convalescent homes at the coast. In 1914, a roof top school at Centaur Road in Earlsdon, was opened for about thirty children with considerable success and children improved with fresh air, milk and a good meal each day.

The Children's Care Committee received £100.00 funding from the council, plus various voluntary contributions. In 1914, they were able to open a Camp School at Corley for ten children on land provided by Miss Cash. It was a simple shack with poor amenities and parents also contributed to the costs. Some children came for the summer, others for a few weeks. The experiment in 'open air life' proved so beneficial that the camp was enlarged to take 16 children. In 1927, a permanent open-air school opened for forty-five girls and forty-five boys.

THE MEMORIES OF CHILDREN

The 'memories' of children attending are in stark contrast to the 'adults' involved with running the school. The regime was rigid and boys seemed to cope less well with being removed from their families than the girls. Parent visiting was limited to once a month. Extracts from reports (below) give a glowing picture of the school. Children had various illnesses and chest problems but the majority suffered from general debility due to a poor diet. This was such a serious national problem that the government had to find measures to improve the health of both children and adults. The answer lay in education, free school meals for the needy and free milk to all children.

Cookery and gardening lessons were introduced into schools' curriculum so boys learnt how to grow their own vegetables and girls learnt how to cook. Within twenty years, there was a marked improvement in the health of children (and the nation).

Open Air Classroom (1928)

Report by Miss Bailey 1919 (Extract)

"The Corley Camp School opened its fifth session on the 3rd May 1919 and closed on 31st October. Certain improvements were made that have been of considerable benefit. A canvas shelter was erected in the field as a playroom. Wet days are no longer a nightmare to the staff, as children have been able to play and have lessons in the shelter instead of crowding into the dormitory among the beds."

Bluebell Picking

"The schoolwork has been very elementary. The average age of children on arrival was nine and a half. Out of 18 children selected for the school, eleven could neither read nor write, except by laborious copying. When the children arrived they looked thin, pale, hollow eyed, forlorn and their attitude apathetic. Within even a month they were very different. During six months, most have outgrown clothes, were rosy, bright eyed, full of energy and interested in everything. These good results have been attained by a plenteous diet of simple, good and varied food, regular hours, much rest and cult of the bath. The schoolroom has always been a scene of cheerful business.

Nature study has been intensely practical. The love of living things has become the central interest of the children's life here. The youngest are often the quickest to discover new flowers or insects. Previously, many children have hardly attended school at all. In six months they may make good headway and a desire to learn. What is to happen if these children remain well enough to return to normal school? They cannot, in a large class, receive the individual attention they still need."

Report by Miss E. Townsend Teacher in Charge 1920 (Extract)

"The change in the children has been marked, both physically and mentally. When they arrived they seemed afraid to express an opinion. After a few days they realised that they had freedom such as they had not known before, and great was the delight when they found the whole field was for their use. Our first visit to the woods was a revelation to me, many had not been to a wood before. Their idea was – the home of the fairies. Corley Moor, was also of great interest, especially when the heather was in bloom.

The children have worn their own clothes, as the jerseys and kilts provided by the Care Committee were mostly worn out. I would like to suggest, that in future, a few night-shirts and night gowns were provided, also a few changes of underclothing, as many children had no extra change, and if a change were necessary, we found it difficult and there have been instances of children remaining in bed while underclothing was washed."

Report by Dr. Newton 1921 (Extract)

"The continued good results by sending children to the open-air school for the summer, point towards an extension of the method as soon as it is financially possible. The practical rebuilding of the large play shed last spring, has made possible, the enlargement of the Camp by using part of this shed as a dormitory. The shelter used as a schoolroom, has been boarded in place of the tarpaulin. We were provided with some desks for the elder children; these, though far from ideal, were very useful, as was a cupboard for school materials. A second bath was fixed and a boarded floor put in the dining shelter.

The work of the Camp has been very interesting and the average increase in weight has been greater than last year. In July, the Mayor appealed through the Press for a gramophone and toys for our use, and we were provided with tennis rackets, cricket sets, skipping ropes and a gramophone. The Governors of Bablake School, very generously presented capes for the children's use, and these have proved very useful indeed. Miss Warden of Rock Farm, invited the children to tea in haymaking time, and Miss Sutton, of Corley School, invited them to an open-air dancing display, and to a 'magic lantern' entertainment.

The ages of the children varied from six to thirteen years. This makes teaching somewhat difficult but the progress of many was very rapid. Some children had only attended school for a few days or months. Parents visited the Camp each month, and most of them expressed their great delight in the children's manner and appearance."

(Eleven children suffered from 'General Debility / Chronic Dyspepsia. Three from Chronic Bronchitis. One from General debility and suspicion of abdominal Tuberculosis.)

Report by Miss Townsend Head Teacher 1927 (Extract)

Girls with cakes (1960c)

"The newly erected Open-Air School opened 26th April 1927. The school is about five miles from Coventry, 600 feet above sea level, in one of the most beautiful parts of Warwickshire. Ninety children arrived aged five to fourteen years. It has a large dining room in the centre, with a boy's dormitory on the west side and girl's dormitory on the east side."

"The three schoolrooms are away from the main building and face south. The old dormitories are converted into an isolation block and manual room for hand-works. The staff comprises of head teacher, three assistant teachers, two trained nurses, cook, two maids and handy man. The school curriculum is the same as in the ordinary elementary school, but the afternoon sessions are devoted to nature study, walks and handwork. This close touch with nature has a wonderful effect on the character of the children. The older boys do woodwork, basketry and gardening and the older girls, leather work, needlework and mending, raffia work and housewifery. The improvement in the children, in spite of a summer without much sunshine and a severe spell of weather in December, has been very wonderful. Not only have they gained weight, but have become alert and bright and now play games without fatigue. This is the first time the school has been open during the winter and it has been in the nature of an experiment. I am pleased to state that colds and coughs have been almost absent and the children have been remarkably fit and happy throughout it all. Our diet is plain but good and includes watercress or lettuce when obtainable, a good supply of fresh milk, an orange per day and cod liver oil."

Report of School Medical Officer (An extract from Dr. Moir's report)

"During 1929, many changes took place in the staff at Corley. The Headmistress, Miss Townsend, died suddenly on 28th August. In September, Miss Page took up the post. Miss Townsend had been associated with Corley Open-Air School from its inception. She had a vigorous but kindly personality."

"A portion of ground by the dining room has been asphalted as a playground. A sewing-maid now visits the school twice a week and the laundry are washed locally instead of, as previously, by the mothers at home. In 1928 and 1929, there was a small epidemic of Scarlet Fever involving 3 boys and 6 girls. During the year, 69 boys and 76 girls were admitted."

The illnesses from which these children were suffering on admission:

Malnutrition:	30
Bronchitis:	22
Rheumatism:	6
Chorea:	13
Valvular disease of the heart:	6
Pleurisy:	2
Dyspepsia:	7
Asthma	3

"The commonest complaint among children is chronic digestive disturbances, which manifest themselves rather differently in children than adults. Ill-balanced meals play a prominent part. The average person remains ignorant on this subject, and of cooking, few have anything beyond an elementary knowledge. The 'cook-shop' is too frequently a refuge and advertisements of this or that artificial food have too much sway.

The Domestic Science Course in schools should assume greater and greater importance for the future well being of the nation. It is easy to put a joint in the oven but how little is known about the preparation of vegetables! The child won't eat them, certainly not; the mother cannot cook them. Corley does its main work in restoring these children to digestive health, which, although un-dramatic, is great as the restoration of movement in a paralysed limb."

Outdoor class (1948) *(Photo by Sunday Mercury)*

History of Corley Open Air School

Dinner Time (1948)
Boy left: Malcolm Warren.
Girl centre: Margaret Norris.
(Photo by Sunday Mercury)

Report in the Birmingham Mercury 12th September 1948 (Extract)

"Ninety kiddies between the ages 5 and 16 are undergoing a 'commando' course at Corley Open-air School, near Coventry, to toughen them for the battle of life. Back in 1918, Coventry Education Committee took over the wooded site as a holiday camp school for delicate and under-nourished children. Since then, permanent buildings have been erected and 8000 kiddies have passed through the school.

The average stay is 17 weeks, and they live within the Coventry city boundary. While most children have chest complaints, no T.B. cases are admitted. Corley School is a great healer. The southerly winds blow straight into the classrooms and dormitories, which stand about 492ft above sea level. The specially-balanced diet includes liberal quantities of milk, fruit, meat, malt and vegetables.

Whenever the weather permits (and the cold doesn't worry them), classes are held in the open-air, and there are frequent picnics. A medical record is kept at the school, temperatures are taken daily and each child is weighed fortnightly.

Corley school is a school with a difference. The head mistress, Miss M.S. Caborn, runs it on ultra-modern lines. Corporal punishment is unknown and there are few restrictions. The only real restriction affects visitors. To avoid the possibility of infection and to prevent homesickness, parents are allowed to see their children once a month only, apart from birthdays, but kiddies are encouraged to write home as often as possible. The records show: Average gain in weight after the course, 8lb. 3oz."

Queen Elizabeth's Coronation celebration (1953)

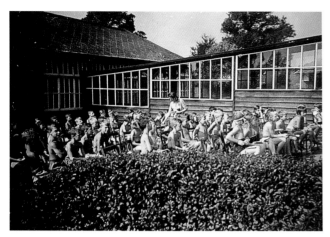

Gwen giving pennies out for Church (1946/7)
(Both photos by Ella Goodman).

Lining up to walk to Church (1946/7)

RESIDENTIAL SCHOOL

In 1944, a new education act said that 'delicate' children should be taught in ordinary schools and the school name was changed to 'Corley Residential School', for children with special needs.

In 1959, the timber school was rebuilt in brick for 120 children. Teaching and communal rooms on the ground floor with sleeping, living and playrooms, (no longer open air) on the first floor. The grounds were planted with many new trees and shrubs. The idea was to make the school more like a home. A child who was continually homesick would be allowed to go home as happy children benefit most from this kind of environment.

CORPORAL PUNISHMENT

Memo 5.9.55. from: Mrs. V. Spencer, Head.
To: Teaching, Nursing Staff and Housemothers.

"Some months ago, I signed a statement, which I sent to the Education Office, to the effect that no member of my staff is allowed to administer corporal punishment. I myself use it only when all other methods have been tried and have failed. Corporal punishment is administered on very rare occasions and then by no other person than my deputy when I am away, or myself. Will you please sign on the back?"

Signed by: Miss R L Stringer, Nurse Lawry, S.R.N. Miss Berry, Miss Wardley, and Miss Bateman, Miss Alldridge, Miss Merry, Nurse Brown, Nurse Fletcher, Miss Louisa, Miss Bruma, Miss Rosa.

Extracts Coventry Evening Telegraph

RUMBLING STOMACHS IN SCHOOL 20/11/1997

One third of pupils in Coventry go to school without having anything to eat for breakfast and one quarter leave home without having had a drink, according to a survey. … Dr. Keith Williams, director of public health for Coventry said "I wasn't that surprised that children went to school without breakfast but I was surprised that a quarter are leaving home without even a drink, so they arrive at school not only starved but dehydrated as well."…

Page 7. By Fiona Scott.

'CAN'T COOK' RISK TO FAMILY HEALTH 2/12/2000

Family health is at risk in deprived areas of Coventry because many people have no idea how to prepare a simple meal, it has been revealed. Councillors considering a food education scheme were horrified to hear that a junk food diet is forced on hundreds of people who don't know the basics of cooking. For many of them obesity is an added problem of 'easy eating.' …

Front page. By Paul Barry.

CORLEY (COVENTRY) SCHOOL - TODAY

(Extract from the School Brochure 1996 - 1997)

The age range of pupils is eleven to sixteen years. The School is for children who experience moderate learning difficulties and for vulnerable children. Corley is both residential and a day school. The grounds cover some six acres and there is a heated indoor swimming pool, an adventure playground, play-area and sports pitch. The classes are smaller than in mainstream schools and we try to make the classroom a happy, stimulating and motivating place. All children have individual needs. This is particularly relevant to the 'Corley' child. He/she will have experienced learning difficulties, and may have some relationship problems with adults or other children and/or be in need of social-skills education. Staff believe that rewarding and praising appropriate behaviour and attitude results in improved behaviour.'

Staff: April 1996 include: Head Teacher: Richard Nason, Deputy: Janet Collins. Teachers: Richard Lewis, Stef Woollacott, Maggie Azarpey, Peter Bell, Pam Burton, Alan Dickey, Rosa Miller, Jason Molloy, Betty Nelan, Norma Tims. Education Asst. Sheila Akhurst, Bernadette Janew, Lisa Radburn.

The Dining Room (1955c)

Corley (Coventry) School (2003)

Maurice Barratt

I was born at 27 Drapers Field, Coventry, in 1924 and was the middle child of five. We had a happy childhood but I was sent to Rhyl Convalescent Home for a month. I played in the sand hills and remember being happy, you could talk and run about and play on swings and seesaws. Staff talked to you and they played music at meal times on a phonograph.

It was a surprise when I was sent to Corley Open Air School for my health. My sister Joan was there already but I hardly ever saw her. My first memory was going to sleep on a canvas bed with wooden legs. The Mistress would shout, "Turn over on your right sides and go to sleep." Often she would stay in a cubicle in the centre of the dormitory, so we just froze and dare not move. In the morning, horror of horrors, the beds were stripped back and if there was a big wet patch, it used to stand out. One poor lad who wet the bed, suffered with his nerves.

The boy's dormitory was at one end and the girls at the other and they kept us well apart. In between were the dining room, sick-bay and all the other little rooms. The dormitory was built of wood and lined with asbestos. One side of the dormitory was open. When there was a gale, they dropped big canvas screens to stop rain blowing in. It would flap and bang about all night.

(1932) Jerry McKennah?, Tom Appleby, Frank Barratt.

PLUCK AT GRASS!

One of the things we did was all sit in a line and pluck the grass in the playing field. It didn't seem a very good occupation then and it still doesn't now! There was very little education. We had some tatty books. The schoolroom had one side open and we would sit on boards. The lack of teaching told on me later.

One day, we were all looking forward to a picnic on the lawn. The headmistress said, "We will sing Grace." We sang the first two lines and she stopped us. We weren't in tune! We tried again and again. In the end, she sent the whole school to bed without any tea. I remember eating liver. You could chew it and chew it and eventually you had to swallow lumps. Every so often they purged us and we had to go and have a cup of sennapod tea. It was pretty horrible. At night they took our temperature and asked us whether we had "been for number ones and number twos?" If you hadn't been, they used to dose you up with some horrible stuff. You soon learnt to say you had been, whether you had or not.

ESCAPE

Parents visited on a Sunday. They brought parcels of food and sweets. Everything was taken off you and shared out. I missed my home and one day, three of us decided to escape. We climbed over the lavatory wall and made a break for it. As we passed the gate the "posse" came out and rounded us up. I think the punishment was no tea. About a week later my father came and put on his stern voice and said that if I did escape, he would bring me straight back. It must have been difficult to keep us there. I think it cost about five shillings a week each.

One day, my father visited me on a weekday. We sat in an alcove and we talked and he gave me a bag of sweets. Later, when we were having our afternoon nap, I undid the bag hidden under the bedclothes. Old 'Hawkeye' was watching and she swooped and took my sweets away.

COUNDON SCHOOL

When I left Corley, I went to a new school in Coundon. I was behind with my lessons and I used to get the cane for not knowing. The teacher didn't try to teach but beat it into me. He had a row of canes and these were named after the Knights of the Round Table. He would let you choose most times. If he didn't, he used to pick Excalibur because it stung more.

At Corley there was indifference and ignorance but no cruelty. You had no adult you could talk to. I think that the only time anyone spoke to me with kindness was when I got German measles.

I have only bad memories although my sister Joan stayed there longer and enjoyed it. She did sewing for them and took the post from school to the post office each afternoon. She was also a monitor. Ten children sat at the same table at meal times and if a child was sick or disliked the meal, Joan had to get a new serving and the child was made to eat it.

Pantomime, Sleeping Beauty 1st left, Tom Appleby. 2nd girl ..Appleby. 3rd left, Arthur Branson. 2nd right, Frank Barratt as wicked witch.

A few years ago, I went up to the main gate at Corley to have a look at the old school, but it had all altered. The buildings were brick and there were children swinging on the gate and playing in front of the building. We were never allowed out the front of the school, apart from when we went to church. Evidently, all the rules had been relaxed since I was there.

Compiled from oral recording (1990)

Margaret Lucus *(nee Hindle)*

Brownies (1950s) Miss Wardle, Brownie Leader.

I was at Corley Open Air school for eighteen months from late 1929. I was aged six and half when I started. I spent two Christmases there and remember the large Christmas tree and one year was delighted to receive a box of dolls house furniture. Our routine was rather strict. We had to eat all the food put in front of us. Cod liver oil was given to us every morning with our porridge. I hated it! The nurse gave it to us and most of the oil would overflow into the porridge! I shudder when I think of it now.

Part of the day we had lessons in the classroom and in the summer we would go out onto the grass. We were also taken for walks around the village. Towards the end of my stay at the school, they started a Brownie pack which I joined. I was in the 'Sprites.'

Compiled from notes written by Mrs. Lucas.

Denis Johnson

I was born in Coventry in 1921. My mother died of tuberculosis when I was 16 months old. After that, I stayed with my aunt who looked after me very well. In 1928, when I developed a bad cough, I was sent to Corley Open Air School in case I had the same illness as my mother. I stayed there during the spring and summer of that year.

I hated being at Corley Open Air School. I didn't like the food, the semolina or the porridge. The nurse was awful! I remember that she was tall, hair pulled back, two projecting front teeth and wore glasses. She made us swallow cod liver oil. She dominated us. The dormitories were open to the air and I slept next to the veranda. It was cold! At night, I could hear strange noises and heavy footsteps in the blackness. I was absolutely terrified and so were other children, consequently there was a lot of bed wetting. One nurse used to shout at the boys in the morning, but no one got the cane.

The head, Miss Paige and the teachers, Miss Bowls and Miss Pinchers, were fine. We went on walks, which I loved, through the blue bell woods and I enjoyed the gardening lessons. My father and aunt would visit on a Sunday and bring me a bag of apples or something. Everything was handed in to be shared out. I dare not tell my father how unhappy I was or I would have had my ears cuffed.

We children, with knowledge of the countryside, used to eat some of the wild plants. We ate new hawthorn leaves, called bread and cheese and the new sorrel shoots as they came through the ground. One of the boys told the nurse so she dragged us into the clinic and gave us a very unpleasant drink, liquorice or something, which went straight through us. Many children ran away from the school and I ran away with a friend, Laurie Biddle. We got as far as Long Lane at Keresley when Miss Paige found us hiding in the hedge. She took us back. Next day, my father came to collect me and took me home.

Compiled from interview (1996)

Family visiting at Corley Open Air School (1928/9)
Harold (cousin), Charlotte (aunt), Denis with brothers Norman and Eric, Father, Thomas Johnson in cap. (He invented the decompressor for the motorbike whilst working on development at Triumph. Previously, bikes had been difficult to start and could cause severe injuries.)

Dean College

I was born December 1935 and sent to Corley Open Air School in November 1941, for eighteen months. My father was a baker and I had one elder brother. We were not poor, but I had a T.B. gland. I had an operative procedure and then sunray treatment at Hartford Hill. After that, they decided to send me to Corley Open Air School to improve my health. I have patchy memories of the school. I remember there were no windows and waking one morning with snow on my bed. The dormitory had a series of shutters that were raised and lowered, but most of the time it was open. I think it did do me good, the food etc. To begin with I found the education very rigid and strict. Visiting was fortnightly. Mothers one week and fathers the other. On Sunday we walked crocodile fashion to Church. There were many outside activities, marching and walking. Many children stayed a long time.

Connie Allinson (nee Northall)

I worked at Corley Residential School as an assistant cook from about 1948, until I retired in 1979. I went as a holiday relief and it just went on from there. It was an 'open air' school. All the dormitories were open. It's a wonder the children didn't freeze to death! The idea was that they had fresh air. It was a silly idea! I thought it was awful. There were no doors on the dormitories, you could see the beds from outside and it used to snow in. As the years went by, they gradually got the nice dormitories and everything improved.

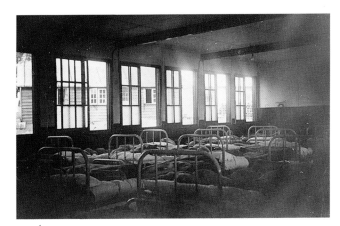

Afternoon rest, boy's dormitory (1947c)

Many children did get better and made very nice grown-ups. Some were poor little things when they came. A few were very backward, but on saying that, some were very thin and poorly with asthma, tuberculosis and other illnesses. You could see them putting the weight on and getting better. For some, the school was good because they were so poor; they didn't know what a nice bed was or a proper meal. Some parents didn't visit and didn't seem to care for them. One little lad, Keith, looked like a little old man and had eczema and something else wrong. He scratched himself all over. He was a poor little soul and didn't live very long. But of course, you didn't get to know all their names as we were in the kitchens.

The children had to work just as they would at an ordinary school in the morning. They came into the big hall for their lunch and then have a rest before they had more schoolwork. I remember one girl, Connie, who came to the school when she was about eleven or twelve. She grew up there and we watched her grow into a nice girl. She got married from the School and my daughter Barbara was her little bridesmaid. There have been many changes and the school is lovely now.

Compiled from oral recording (1999)
Further extract in Fillongley chapter.

Staff at Corley Residential School (1960's)
Back Row: Eddie Wright - Van driver, Sheila Green, Hilda Waugh, Olive Veritage, Gladys Smith, George - odd jobs. Centre Row: Winnie Eglis, Winnie Platt, Connie Allinson, Daisy Watts, Ivy Phillips, Bet Knap, (?), Nancy West. Front row: Ivy Foy, Mary Glover, Ivy Swain, Miss Hallowell - Bursar, Mrs. Spencer - Headmistress, Mr. James - Caretaker, Mrs. James, Sally Mathews, Joyce Glover.

Sophie Edwards

Children playing in sand pit (1947c)
(photo by Ella Goodman)

Staff Accommodation Green Block *Daisy Watts in door.*

PUPIL AND HEADMISTRESS

I was born in 1932. When I went to Corley Open Air School, no one thought it strange to remove children from all contact with their family. I thought it was wonderful. I have happy memories. I think I was mothered and I was younger than the other children. Not a family existence but institutionalised. We went round in large groups. We had to do bomb shelter drill, going with our eyes closed to get used to the blackout.

I returned as Head Mistress, in 1986. It brought back memories. All the buildings were brick built except for one old wooden one, which was knocked down a year after I came. It was like coming to a different school. Children go home weekends and holidays. The children that come to Corley School now, need something more than a normal education. Within the context of this school, they can achieve great things. Some children go into further education, others get jobs straight away.

It was good to have happy memories. Nice to feel that there is a tradition of helping children that has gone back some seventy years or more and that I have been able to continue it.

Joyce Buck *(nee Hancox)*

When my daughter was three, I worked at 'Corley Open Air School' as a cleaner. The headmistress was Mrs. Spencer. This was in 1958 when it was no longer 'open air' but had proper bedrooms and house parents. I stayed for a few years and then returned for another ten years, until my retirement in 1987. I liked working there and my sister also worked there in the kitchens.

The staff were very caring and looked after the children well. They had good food, three cooked meals a day.

When the children came, they were all poorly, some with asthma, eczema or a disability. Some came from very poor backgrounds. Not all of the children got better. They could be very difficult and most did not appreciate the school or the work that the staff did. Some children were terrible! I don't know who was the worst; boys or the girls and the staff were not allowed to smack them for bad behaviour. The domestic science teacher washed one boy's mouth out with carbolic soap for bad language!

See also memories in Corley School Chapter.

Mary Brown (nee Gavan)

STAFF MAID

In 1953, when I was seventeen, I went to work at Corley Residential School as a Staff Maid. The nurses and teachers had a nice dining room and I served breakfast, lunch etc. I also had to help the house mothers wash the boys if there were a lot of wet beds. I think some children may have been a bit traumatised. The bed-wet children had to get up first so that they could be showered and their clothes changed. The teachers and housemothers never said anything about it. The housemothers would shout if the boys got out of bed at night – but that's no different to children at home. No child was ever hit.

The dormitories were still all open-air and I was quite shocked when I first went to the school. They had big shutters to pull down if the weather was really bad. I thought it must be a normal thing to harden the children off and didn't question it. Attitudes were still a bit Victorian then. The children seemed very thin, what I would class from poor or deprived backgrounds. A few may have been taken away for their own safety. The sick bay was always full of children with asthma and those that needed bed-rest. When very delicate children first arrived at the school, they stayed in the sick bay for a week or two before going into the open dormitories.

I think there must have been an improvement in the children before they went home. For some, it may have been their first experience of good meals on a regular basis. A huge pan of porridge was cooked in the morning for their breakfast and there was always fresh vegetables and meat.

All the staff were really nice to work with and lovely to the children. The teachers were very good. Mr. Jones was always there for them and Miss Wardle played with the children, even in the snow! The dining room floor was brown lino and Mrs. Prescott polished it to perfection! On really wet days, the children played in here and had games and comics and things. Occasionally children would abscond across the fields, boys mainly and teachers and senior staff had to search for them and bring them back.

I lived at the school in the Green Block. I had a bedroom, little sitting room and shared a toilet and sink. The bathroom was in Yellow Block. All the domestic staff ate in the kitchen. My mother was the evening Cook, so she cooked supper for me and I saw her every day. I left in 1955, when I got married and moved to Coventry. They were very happy days.

Compiled from interview (2002)
Further extract in Corley chapter.

Staff at Corley Open Air School (1953)
Back row: (Van driver), (?), Mrs. Vi Garret, Elsie Ball, Elsie Eeglis, Hilda Wolf, Barbara Holt, Mrs. Beatrice Gavan, Winnie Platt, Nurse Flether, Mrs. Gladys Scattergood, Connie Grimmett, Mrs. Prescote, (? Seamstress), Mrs. Connie Allinson, Mrs. Chadband, Mrs Daisy Watts, Mrs. Edith Wright, George - handyman. Front Row: Mary Gavan, Miss Bruna, Mrs. Batman, Miss Wardle, (?), (?), Mrs. Parker - Head Teacher retiring, Miss Spencer - New Head-Teacher, Mrs. Brown, Miss Stringer, Mr. Jones, Miss Berry, Miss Louisa, Mrs. James.

Sheila Barley

I went to work at Corley Residential School in September 1963. Mr. Ron Ottley was the head teacher and he was very nice and a good head. There were a variety of children. Some were educationally slow, some generally naughty that no one could deal with, others were delicate children with heart problems and asthma. We had a nurse and a small sick bay and they had their treatment for skin eczema, bed wetting, epilepsy and others were referred for treatment to the hospitals.

The children went home for holidays and they came from all over the country. Some children got better. Some left when they were older. Some were from very poor homes. The delicate children were quite surprisingly noisy and exuberant. At one time it was an open air school in the fields, but that had finished. There were four house parents for the girls and more for the boys. House parents and teachers had flats or bed sitting rooms. None of the children were confined to bed. They were taught maths, English, craft, art, drama, singing, games, geography, history, home economics, cooking, sewing, pottery and gardening. Outings were also arranged. Each Christmas we put on a pantomime and in the summer a garden party and fair. Every Sunday we went to Corley Church.

Sometimes children would run away, when they had just come back after the holidays and were unsettled or because it was a means to try and get their own way. We had to notify the police and go round searching for them. Corley Residential School was a beautiful place and a very good school. I look in the papers and sometimes see the boy's names, getting married and having children. Some have died and some of the naughty ones have ended up in prison.

Compiled from interview (1990)

Judith Raven *(nee Yaxley)*

I have very fond memories of my time at Corley Residential School. I went there in 1956 when I was nine, for twelve weeks. My father had Tuberculosis and my younger sister had an attack which was being treated. I know Mum must have found the financial circumstances very difficult as dad was ill for three years. Looking back at photos of myself, I was very thin and I thought we were all there to be fattened up a bit! Obviously, there was more to it but I wasn't aware of any problems.

We all slept in large dormitories, which looked like a huge barn. The uniform was issued army style and I can remember the arms of my jumper, (both issues) were far too short. I knew my arms were long but my jumpers always made the problem worse! We queued up for our daily 'dose' of malt which I grew to love, but for one friend, it made her mornings after breakfast a real misery.

Compiled from notes written by Judith Raven (1999)

EXTRACT FROM 'CORLEY PARISH NEWS LETTER' CHRISTMAS 1955

A boy swallowed a stone and had to be rushed off to hospital. The Head was away and on her return, Mrs. Spencer enquired to the reason for the accident. It was then learned that he had swallowed one stone but the other boys would not believe him. So he promptly swallowed another, and to make things perfectly clear, he ended his strange meal with a dice! (The boy was John Jones).

Mr Jones and the gardening class (1950's)

CHAPTER FIVE

Fillongley School & House (1982)

FILLONGLEY SCHOOL

Fillongley has a long history, dating back more than one thousand years and has the remains of two castles. The parish is large with scattered settlements typical of the old Forest of Arden and place names include Green End, Wood End and Chapel Green. Fillongley was said to provide everything a person could need without going out of the parish. In 1850, there were five inns and taverns, two beer houses, two butchers, three blacksmiths, three bricklayers, three carpenters, one cattle dealer, two dress makers, one woodturner, four corn millers, forty five farmers, five grocers, two malsters, two saddlers, seven shoemakers, three surgeons, four tailors, one timber merchant, two wheelwrights etc. A number of charities provided for the poor of the parish and few people were sent to the workhouse at Meriden. The village had parish houses and gave simple employment, including hedge cutting and road sweeping, to men who had become disabled so that they could support their families.

CHARITY BOYS DRESSED IN GREEN AND BLUE SUITS

Fillongley was fortunate to have a very early charity school. Ayliffe Green of Gloucester, bequeathed land in Fillongley in 1690, to pay towards the cost of a schoolmaster in Fillongley and Arley. Ten poor boys aged seven to fourteen, were taught reading, writing and accounts and given a green suit, cap, two shirts and two pairs of shoes. The charity continued to provide green suits into the early twentieth century. The early classroom would probably be a room in the house where the master or mistress lived. Other village children could receive a basic education by paying a penny or two each week.

William Avery, lived at Slowley Hall and left land in 1732 so that another ten poor boys could be educated and clothed in blue suits. Any surplus rents were used to pay for apprenticeships for poor children. The children of Fillongley did not benefit from this charity for more than forty years due to a claim to the property and protracted litigation.

AEMILLIAN HOLBECHE - THE BLACK SHEEP

The Holbeche family, from the days of the de Hastings of Fillongley Castle, had been entrusted to manage affairs in the village. Unfortunately, one black sheep was AEmillian Holbeche. In 1772, he nominated a trustee to manage and recover the William Avery charity lands. With little or no control from the other trustees, he personally took over the management of the charity and became bailiff and treasurer and doubled his salary, from ten to twenty guineas a year. He claimed, that due to the costs of litigation, he needed to personally occupy Slowley Hall and receive rents from the land. A large amount of money that should have been available for the charity was kept in his own account, although some money was received and 13 apprentices placed between 1817 – 1826, at a cost of £118. It was not until Holbeche's death in 1832 that the scandal was revealed and proper control was taken by the vicar and trustees.

GIRLS TO LEARN ENGLISH, KNITTING & SEWING

Richard Walker bequeathed Walker's Farm and land in Fillongley in 1754, to provide for a schoolmaster to teach boys who were not provided for by the Ayliffe Green charity. He also provided for a schoolmistress to teach girls to read English, to knit and do plain sewing. William Walmsley bequeathed the residue of his personal estate for charitable purposes, for whatever his trustees thought fit. His trustees and Rev. John Thickens, in 1826 considered that the schoolmistress, provided for under Walkers Charity, needed more support. This meant that all village girls, aged between six and twelve, could attend school if they wished to.

Compiled from Charities Government Report.

Ayliffe Cottage, formerly known as the Dame School

DAME SCHOOL

A school was built in 1779 on land given by Henry Garner. This became known as the 'Dame School.' From the 1844 Tithe Map, the mistress of the girl's school was Sophia Jones and the house belonged to Walker's Charity. Sophia Jones was still teaching at the school in the 1870's and children not provided for by the charities, could pay a penny or two each week to attend school.

The Charities were combined in 1912, to form 'Fillongley Educational Foundation,' and it is still in existence today. The Dame School was rented and occupied for many years by a village blacksmith, Thomas Keatley and his wife ran a tearoom from the cottage. It was sold in 1958 and Nigel Laurence Holbeche, a Chartered Surveyor, made a Statutory Declaration that for at least forty years there had never been a dispute to its ownership.

1840 THE SUNDAY SCHOOL

In 1840, land was given by Lord Leigh and the first and largest room of the Sunday School was paid for by Joseph Johnson. The sole condition was that the classroom was never to be converted to any other use or purpose. A new room was added in 1877 to make an Infants School.

For many years, a blacksmith's was sited next to the Sunday school. In 1870, Thomas Hubbard was blacksmith followed by Jacob Hubbard who was deaf and dumb. In 1921, the smithy was demolished to build a third room. Above the window of the room can be seen the design of a large horseshoe, in blue bricks, in memory of the blacksmiths. In 1984, the Sunday school was no longer required, so plans were made to convert it into two bungalows. A furious campaign to save the Sunday School was mounted by village residents. The Educational Foundation agreed not to sell it but to let it to the Parish Council at a peppercorn rent. This was fortunate, as it was integrated into the new Bournebrook School.

1876-7 THE VICTORIAN SCHOOL

The 1844 Tithe Map shows that adjacent to the Dame School were three houses, a schoolroom and yard, owned by Fillongley Church Wardens. The school must have been small and inadequate and was demolished about 1879, when a new school was built. The proceeds from the sale of materials were used to aid the building of the school and the small patch of ground (in front of the Church) was turned into a flowerbed and war memorial. The attractive Victorian school and schoolhouse were built around 1876-7. Tenders for the work were received from builders: Matthews - £2,100. Marriott - £2,075. Nelson - £1,994. Nightingale & Downes - £1,826. The lowest tender was accepted. The architect was John Cotton of Birmingham and Bromsgrove. The school is typical of his architectural design. To oversee his work, he would have had to travel from Bromsgrove to Fillongley, using the steam train to Arley Station.

Book on John Cotton: by Jennie McGregor-Smith. Source: Builders News 13/7/1877.

REDUCING NUMBERS

Fillongley School always had a good reputation and provided an education for children from infants to school leavers. It was three separate schools in one: infants, girls and boys. The headmaster lived in the schoolhouse and it was not uncommon for his wife and daughters to teach in the school.

With better educational standards required by governments during the 20th century, Fillongley did not have the amenities to keep pace with the changing times. In 1948, children from the age of eleven were sent to Herbert Fowler, the senior school, in Old Arley. The school numbers were again reduced in the 1960's, when children from the age of eight were taken by bus to Herbert Fowler as it changed to a middle school. Senior children were transported by bus to Alderman Smith in Nuneaton.

For the remaining infant children, a new flat roofed building was erected, not at all in keeping with the village or Victorian School architecture. School numbers continued to dwindle, due to smaller families.

Side view of Fillongley School with bell tower (1920c)

In 1995, Corley and Fillongley Schools were given notice to close. Both communities combined forces and campaigned to save at least one school. The County Council agreed, but would not make the decision over which school should close. The combined Boards of Governors, chaired by Cllr. Ian Blythe, for Fillongley and Mrs. Ann Evans, for Corley, came to the difficult decision that Fillongley was the better site.

BOURNEBROOK SCHOOL

Work on an attractive extension to join the 1960's building with the Victorian school was completed in August 1996. Improved facilities include a library, gymnasium, extra classrooms, kitchen and head teacher's study. The new school caters for nursery children and for children aged four to eleven. The numbers increased from under 40 to 120. The headmistress, who undertook the task of combining the two schools, was Mrs. Anne Pipe. The school is named after the stream that meanders by Fillongley Castle, culverts under the main road and emerges again behind the school.

Work starts on the new school, amalgamating the old Victorian school with the 1960's building (January 1996)

The new Bournebrook School extension

Rev. David W. Barr

My parents were married in 1814 and had eight children. I opened my eyes on the world on March 18, 1831, in a scattered hamlet called Wood End. My father was a shoemaker and my mother supplemented his earnings by silk ribbon weaving on a handloom, which was a commonplace occupation in the cottage homes. They attended a Nonconformist place of worship and this aroused a feeling of bitterness and the patronage of the Church people was withdrawn, so my father had to travel miles distant in search of orders.

At an early age I was put to a Dame's School, but my real school days commenced when I was seven years of age. The school was situated at Fillongley and was conducted in a large irregular-shaped room over several parish houses. It was common to see 'Parish House,' painted over a cottage door here and there. Cottages were bought or rented by the guardians to provide free shelter for those in need.

The master was a quaint looking man about fifty or sixty years of age, stout and podgy, having a very large head, and standing only about four feet six inches high. He had a soft and flabby hand, but could use it to purpose in applying a holly-stick to the palms of defaulting pupils. I do not remember that I ever received a lesson in grammar during the whole time spent at school. Indeed, I question if the master himself was competent to give instruction in a subject which was quite outside the curriculum of village schools in those days.

The school being endowed by an ancient charity, my education never cost my parents a penny beyond a small outlay in books, which were very few and inexpensive. Some of the poorest boys were provided with jackets, caps and breeches – some blue, others green. On leaving Fillongley School at the age of twelve, I had a great desire for further tuition and my mother took me to Dr. Sheepshanks, Principal of Coventry Grammar School, but finding that the fees were beyond her means, we returned home with sad hearts. Instead, I was compelled to leave home to earn my living.

Compiled from an autobiography by Rev. D.W. Barr. 'Climbing the Ladder.' (Birmingham Record Office).

Helena Briggs (nee Nellie Sewell)

I was born in 1900 and moved from Yardley to the Windmill at Corley. When we visited my granddad at Sheldon, we had to walk to Meriden to meet the carrier's cart. My mother would take a freshly killed chicken, which she then plucked, whilst walking along. I attended Fillongley School from the age of five until I left when I was fourteen, to enter service. Miss Foote was the Head Mistress and Miss Stevens the teacher. The boy's Headmaster was Mr. Peter Kay. The lads used to sing: "Peter Kay is a very good man, tries to teach us all he can, reading, writing, arithmetic and never forgets to give us the stick!"

The Reading Room, next to the school, was used for both the girl's cookery lessons and the boy's carpentry lessons. There were no books in there so I don't know why they called it the Reading Room? The girls also learnt how to make patchwork quilts. For a special treat after Church on Good Friday, we visited the Vicarage for hot cross buns. In bad weather, I wore wood clogs to school and these were put by the school stove to dry. On my way to school, one of my jobs was to collect firewood. I would leave it in various places ready for picking up on my way home. I would carry it in my pinafore across the fields. At home, I always knew when a pig was going to be killed as a bench was placed in position in the yard. I would go early to school on that day!

Some Saturday mornings, I earnt a penny from the Peaks at Park Farm, scaring rooks and crows with a rattle. We children also did the hay turning and one day, after finishing, it rained. I cried, as we would have to do it all again the next day. One boy nearly died as he tried to find a tunnel to Fillongley Castle. He crawled underground near the brook and was overcome by bad air. He was dragged out by several other boys. The village constable came and made it 'out of bounds.'

Compiled from notes written by Mrs. Helena Briggs.

Beatrice Harris

I was born in 1906 and when I first went to Fillongley School, I thought Miss Foote, the headmistress, very peculiar. I found out afterwards that her glasses were tinted blue. I passed an exam and went to the Pupil Teacher Centre at Nuneaton High School with Eileen Taylor and another girl who died. My sister went with Pat Ibbotson to Nuneaton Girls High School. We used to race along to catch the train in the morning. I started teaching in 1924. At first, I cycled to work, and then I got a Francis Barnett motorcycle. It was a horrible thing! You could hear me 'popping' along! I first taught at Bedworth, then at a girl's school in Stockingford. I also taught at Corley Village School for a while.

Oral recording by Bill Bolton and Bernard Tranter (1981)

Fillongley School (1912c)
Left: Miss Foote. Right: Miss Stevens. Back row: 5th Ethel Hubbard?
Centre Row: Nellie Sewell, Maud Hodges, (?), Ethel Wagstaff, Annie Meek. Front Row: Alice Sewell, (?), (?), Ada? Hubbard?

Pat Ibbotson

My father was educated at Fillongley Dame School. He walked from Gun Hill and he said he sat under the table and didn't get much of an education. I was born in 1910 and we lived at the Manor House in Fillongley, which my father rented, for £30. a year. My mother didn't want me to go to the village school so the Miss Rileys gave me lessons. When I was seven, it couldn't be helped, I went to school. I was too old for the infants and Mrs. Kay was ill, so the school was left in charge of Miss Mary Kay. The younger children were put into one room, which was partitioned, and I had these younger children to look after. I was told to smack them if they were naughty, so I did. The result was that I had to run the gauntlet of all their older brothers and sisters, so Mummy had to meet me and it didn't endear me to the rest of the village.

I was eight when the First World War began. I had three brothers in the war. Hughie got shot down over France. The Seaton's lost four sons. Two came home and took a long time to die. I remember a cloud over us. When the Armistice came, there was a bad influenza epidemic and I don't remember any celebrations. I was off school for seven weeks. The church bell seemed to be ringing most of the time for the deaths. I went up to the girls school when I was eight, under Miss Foote, the headmistress. She used the cane but I never got it. My mother said that if I ever did, there would be a row. I was transferred to Nuneaton High School when I was ten. That meant a walk of five miles a day. When I was fifteen, five of us passed a Candidates Examination to teach, which was the last thing I wanted to do but it managed to keep me at school until I was eighteen. I then got a major scholarship. I think we were quite an interesting group, there were five of us in the sixth form and we were the first people ever to do science.

Miss Ibbotson taught at Barrs Hill School for many years.
Oral recording by Bill Bolton and Bernard Tranter (1981)
See also book: Strawberries & Sewage.

Bob Scatergood

I was born in 1908 in the old Mormon Chapel House in Broad Lane, Fillongley. We kept moving to larger houses, as the family kept getting bigger. Miss Kay was our first teacher. We learnt phonetically. We learnt the vowels and then we put the consonants with them. Ba La Ca. It was surprising how quickly we learnt. We learnt to write on slates for quite a long time because you could rub them out. As you went through the years, you got to Mr. Kay. He was a strict man. I got the stick several times. I was one of a twin and we were known as the terrible twins. If we did anything wrong, we would both get the cane. My brother used to have bad chilblains on his fingers and my mother swore at Mr. Kay. She told him not to cane his hands but to cane his ass!

Compiled from oral recording (1987)
See also book: Strawberries & Sewage.

Mrs. Spencer (nee Parker)

ASSISTANT TEACHER 1911

I came to Fillongley in September 1911, to be an assistant teacher at Fillongley Boys School. I had a letter from Rev. Stevens, asking me to meet him at Stratford upon Avon. He said that he had only just been appointed as Chairman of the School Managers and knew nothing about what questions he should ask me. I was in the same position so he decided that as I had the qualifications, I should be appointed. The headmaster arranged for me to lodge with Mr. and Mrs. Ensor in the Bakehouse.

To reach Fillongley from Leamington Spa, I decided to go by train to Coventry and to walk to where Mr. Coton, the carrier, left his cart at an Inn. His cart consisted of a covered wagon with benches along three sides. As a newcomer, my seat was at the back - the two most important customers sat at the front with the driver. It took us two hours to go six miles because Mr. Coton had to call at various farms and houses to deliver articles he had brought for the residents, or repairs he had done, and of course, he must pass the time of day!

There was no electricity or gas in Fillongley. Houses were lit by lamps and you had a candle to light you to bed. At first, I was very nervous of lamps, as I had been used to gaslights. We had quite a walk to church on dark nights and the way you could tell you were on the road, was by watching the tops of the hedges.

There were three separate schools. Each department had its own classrooms and primitive outside toilet block. Mr. Kaye was Headmaster of the boys, Miss Foote, Headmistress for the girls and Mrs. Kaye, Headmistress of the infants. There were about 80 boys, 80 girls and 50 infants. The children spoke very well and there was no accent. At the end of the day, the headmaster walked to the door and every boy saluted him as they passed by and the girls had to curtsey to the headmistress.

Miss Parker (later Mrs Spencer)

I was given the small classroom, for which I was grateful, as I was able to adjust myself. It held 20 - 30 boys in desks of four, with footrest but no backs. They each had four little holes for inkwells. The room had a good fireplace and plenty of coal, but as the fire went out after school and was not lit until eight o'clock next morning, we had to do quite a lot of physical jerks on cold mornings.

NATURE STUDY

We grew plants in the windows. One morning I found my onions, that were growing in Bovril bottles, had burst because the water had frozen. During summer months, the heat was dreadful. One very hot day when the School Inspector came, he said that it was like the black hole of Calcutta. I had a very happy time with the boys. I thought that in a village, nature study was nearest to them, so we had a nature chart and the boy who brought the first flower had his name on the chart. The boys became very keen and would consult the flower book to see if they had found a different flower. The Managers (through the headmaster) bought us an aquarium, made by Mr. Keatley, the blacksmith. We went to the pool opposite for newts, beetles and water boatmen. From the brook we got shrimps, minnows and sticklebacks.

CONTENTS OF SANDWICHES

I was amazed at the contents of the sandwiches. Sliced turnips and beetroot were brought for dinner, but they enjoyed them. There was a big iron kettle in school so I decided to boil water and make an Oxo drink. I also cooked potatoes. The boys would bring large potatoes with their initials cut into them. I put them under the fire and there was a lovely smell of roast potatoes.

When I went to teach at the infant school, the bottom pane of each window was thick fluted glass. When two of them were broken, I was allowed plain glass on condition that I did not waste time watching people passing by. On wet days, boots were placed round the curb of the fire and stockings on the iron guard to dry. One day, a boy was late and I put his boots too close to the fire. At night, the soles of the boots had parted company with the tops. I wrote a letter to his mother and she came the next day to the Headmaster, who gave her some money for a new pair.

Fillongley School (1922)
Back Row: Mary Carr, Mary Parker, Jennie Paice, Edie Anderton, Winnie Fowdry, Ruth Taylor. Centre Row: Annie Parker, Alice West, Elsie Tedds, Harriet Meek, Alma Evrall, Annie Garner, Annie Meek, Doris Beale, May Scattergood, Florrie Sears. Front Row: Lily Billingham, Martha McCarthy, May Shaw, Rowena Ismay, Mary Craner, Gwen Jester, Emily Shaw.

We taught reading, writing, arithmetic, drawing, history, geography, and object lessons. Object lessons involved a discussion about anything, e.g. a lump of coal. The children achieved a high standard. In those days the retarded child was kept back in the lowest grades. Each child had a class book (7-8 years) (9-10 years) (11-14 years). This was a standard workbook, which had to be worked through completely before they could proceed to the next class. We had no poetry books so I had to write a copy of a poem for each child to learn. A few years ago, a man aged 70, recited a whole poem I taught him when he was ten. History consisted of stories from the Romans up to present. Geography, learning names of capes, bays, rivers, countries with towns and their most important industries. We did drill or exercises and played football and cricket. We went into the next field for football through the fence with a missing rail. I was rather plump and things were tense as to whether I could get through the opening.

RATS ATE THE CHOCOLATE

Scripture lessons lasted half and hour each day, each class had its own part of the catechism to learn by heart. Every week the vicar came to School to give a lesson to the children. At Christmas, we had a party with a tea and games. The local doctor was Father Christmas and he also gave a conjuring performance. The Christmas tree was presented by Mr. and Mrs. Adderley from Fillongley Hall. One year, the tree caught fire and the vicar acted as the fire brigade. Another year, the rats ate most of the chocolate presents.

FROGS, NEWTS AND BEE KEEPING

Mr. Kaye was a keen beekeeper and he had hives at the bottom of his garden. One year, the bees had gathered so much honey that the top of the hive reached the shelf and they had no more space. The bees got very cross. Before Mr. Kaye could do anything about it, the School Inspector arrived. To my dismay, I saw the Inspector running up the playground, chased by bees. Another year, Mr. Kay decided the boys should be taught about bee keeping. He brought in a big zinc tub with a rod down the middle and a rope fastened to the top. On the rod, he fixed the honey-combs and the boys pulled the rope making the honey fly from the combs. The empty combs were given to the boys to eat. When the caretaker came in, she was very annoyed to find honey everywhere. The caretaker had another unpleasant experience when my newts went for a stroll and she refused to remove them from the floor! Luckily she was not in when the tadpoles changed into frogs and jumped from the two jars on the window, causing pandemonium among the children who had to catch them and take them to the local brook

Fillongley School (1910c)
Left: Miss Bell and Miss Stevens? Right: Mr. Kay, (Headmaster).

During World War One, we collected dandelion roots and there was also a request for foxglove seeds. The school had a half-acre allotment strip and the bigger boys and the headmaster, went to work there. Each boy had a plot and grew his own vegetables with great pride. Every morning at 8.50 a.m., the bell in the school belfry was rung for 5 minutes. It was my task to give the signal but if I was a minute or two late, the headmaster took out his watch and told me that people set their clocks by the school bell.

Once a year, the boys assembled in the playground near the school and the Headmaster walked along looking at boots. I do not know how the children knew, but on that day a considerable number of children were wearing very worn boots. One of the charities provided new boots and the boys chosen were sent to Mr. Batchelor's house to be measured for a new pair. Another charity provided green and navy suits for boys whose parents were in poor circumstances.

During the Second World War, our school was very full. Some Coventry teachers came with the children. The men of the village made an underground air raid shelter at the bottom of the playground. We only tried it once but we knew it was there if we wanted it. A boy from Coventry who had just lost his mother stayed with me for two years. I had a letter from Queen Elizabeth thanking me for taking care of him.

Headmasters: Mr. Kaye retired 1922. Mr. Bartlett left 1936. Mr. Whittaker left 1949. Miss Townsend 1950-59. Mrs. Spencer retired in 1956. Compiled from memories written by Mrs. Spencer.

Dewis (Spuggy) Parkes

I was born at Crossways Cottages in 1918. My father was a miner at the 'Tunnel,' Galley Common. I was about four when I started school and Mrs. Spencer was my first teacher. Mr. Darling was very strict. I didn't like school and I used to go round to Fillongley Garage to work instead of going to school. Mrs. Spencer's husband owned Fillongley Garage and the truant officer didn't come round to me. Most of the time, my parents didn't know I missed school.

Compiled from oral recording (1999)

Connie Allinson (nee Northall)

My mother was Sarah Meek and her parents kept the Butchers Arms in Fillongley. My dad was Thomas Northall and there were thirteen children in his family. I was born in 1917 and we lived in Crossways Cottages where I stayed all my life until recently. I had an older sister, Frances and a brother, Sidney. I don't remember my brother as he died of pneumonia when he was little. He liked to play under the water pump and get wet.

We had no water or electricity and there was one water pump to ten cottages. The toilets were down the yard in blocks of three and it was a terrible job emptying them. Men grumble about jobs today but they wouldn't have liked that job! My dad used to work at the pit and we got coal, so that was all right. We managed because you didn't know anything different. There were no 'mod-cons.' Life is better today.

My first teachers were Mrs Kay and Mrs. Spencer. We learnt to write on little slates with chalk. Then we had inkwells and pens with nibs. I liked cookery and domestic science. I liked everything about school. You go and you learn and that's the way of going on. Mr. Bartlett was headmaster, he was nice and lived in the schoolhouse.

Thomas Northall, Francis, Mrs. Sarah Northall (nee Meek), Connie (1920c)

When I was in the 'big' class, they used to fetch me out to do some jobs in the house. His wife was a bit of a 'la-di-da' and I don't think she liked housework. I think that's why he put on my school report that I was good at domestic science.

Compiled from oral recording (1999)
See further extract in Corley Open Air School chapter.

Fillongley School (1932c)
Back row: (?), Harold Lee, Mary Butler or Ida Lowe, Cynwyd Williams, Colin Matthews, Ernie Glover?, Peter Price. Centre Row: Mary Farmer, Pearl Bailey, (?), Muriel Pearman, (?), Doris King, (?), Rhoda Matthews, (?), Elthel Kelsey. Front Row: Gordon Wright, (?), Albert Rose, Blanche Fulford, (?), Bill Daft, (?), Ruby Ward, Kathleen Martin, Leslie Goode, Peter Wood.

David Ives

I was born on the outskirts of Fillongley Parish in August 1920, in an old 16th Century farmhouse known as Brock Hall. It was then two cottages and had rather primitive facilities. Fresh water was obtained from the spring, fenced round in the meadow, bucketed out by my mother. The cooking range was fuelled by coal and we sometimes used a primus stove. The lighting was paraffin oil lamp and candles. The privy (toilet) was some 20 yards down the garden and the washing and boiling of our clothes was done in the 'copper' in the back kitchen. Shawbury Industrial School was half a mile away and I remember hearing the trumpet or bugle call for 'reveille and lights out' at the school. The boys marched to Fillongley Church on a Sunday morning, in time with the School Brass Band. I believe the headmaster was Mr. Craven Jones.

I started Fillongley School in 1925. My mother took me at first on the back of her bicycle. Later, I went with older children and we used to go in a group, picking up the odd child, here and there, on the way. In the winter we used the longer route via the lanes and a two-mile walk. In the summer we walked across fields, which were ablaze with wild flowers. We caught the train from Arley Station to Nuneaton. We pushed a handcart with pram wheels to bring back shopping from Nuneaton.

I frequented the village shop close to the school, spending my two-pence per week pocket money, usually on sherbet bags and liquorice. Mrs. Spencer, a very kindly lady, taught us in the lower classes. Later we were taught by Miss Green and Mr. Bartlett, the Headmaster. I can almost smell the scent now of wet mackintoshes and carbolic soap in the cloakroom. My proud possession was a silver, shield shaped badge with the Bear and Ragged Staff (County Emblem) I received as class prefect or monitor, democratically elected by the class. This I had to relinquish when I was ten as we went to live in Newport, Salop. I look back with nostalgia, of very happy, contented days in Fillongley.

Compiled from notes written by David Ives.

Vera Robinson (nee Steeley)

My father was a Master Carpenter and he worked for the Gazeys for a few years. We lived at Wood End and I attended Fillongley School, 1928 to 1932. Children who lived too far to walk home, took sandwiches or in winter, a large potato, carved with our initials and these were put underneath the boiler ashes to cook.

We played lots of games. Girls played hopscotch with a flat piece of stone or blocks of wood. We all played marbles. It was a summer game; down on the ground we crouched, rolling marbles into a hole gouged in the hard sandy soil, flattened by many feet. Everyone played with hoops. The metal hoops could be bought but most used bicycle rims or hoops off barrels, hit with a stick and bowled round the playground. No balls were allowed to be kicked or thrown, so girls played by hitting balls against the wall and bouncing them on the ground. Skipping was a girl's game, skipping alone or in a group - if someone brought a long rope. There were lots of skipping rhymes. 'All in a bottle of gin. All out a bottle of stout,' or, 'As I was in the kitchen doing a bit of stitching, in came a beggar man and pushed me out.' One of my favourite group games was 'For we are the English.' The boys called it, 'Are you ready for a fight?'

The whole playground of children would be in one of two lines, facing each other. A line was drawn down the centre and after a noisy argument as to which side would be which, the game commenced. Holding hands, one line would advance towards the other and retreat, with repeated singing.

MAXSTOKE SCHOOL AND BURDOCK WINE

We left Fillongley and moved to Maxstoke for several years. It was a very small village school and I remember playing a lot. In the field next to the school, we picked burdocks and gave them to the headmistress so that her mother could make wine from them. Next we moved to Arley and I went to Gun Hill School. The mistress realised my arithmetic had been neglected and she kept me in to teach me, so I could catch-up before I moved to Herbert Fowler - the senior school. I would have liked to go to a grammar school but there weren't many opportunities for village children in those days.

Compiled from interview and notes written by Vera Robinson.

Joan Watts (nee Morris)

My parents, Leslie and Sylvia Morris, ran the Saracens Head at Corley Ash from 1921 to 1932. I went to Fillongley School and it was a happy place. My first teacher was Mrs. Spencer, a nice motherly lady. Miss Kay was my next teacher; she was very strict and I learnt my times tables with her. Two children, Kathleen and Billy who lived with their mother in a barn at Ismay's farm, were the poorest people I have ever known. My mother used to swear we caught head lice off them and other mothers must have felt the same, so no one wanted to sit by them in school. We walked to school in all weathers and the roads were little better than cart tracks. Daimler Cars used the road to test their cars. If they offered us a lift, we politely said, 'no thank you.'

I had piano lessons and, as children, we used to put on concerts. One day we were singing, 'Mr. Baggy Breeches,' when our Airedale dog ran off with the box of money we had taken at the door. We all ran after him, leaving the audience to themselves! My father was secretary of the Corley Horticultural Society and with his legal training, helped many farmers. My mother, with assistance from Mrs. Shay, Mrs Hutt and others, used to organise special dinners for the farmers and miners and Christmas and harvest dinners. Mrs. Hutt was a very large lady and she cycled from Wood End on a sit-up and beg bicycle, her buttocks over-lapping the saddle! There was also the trip to Blackpool and the Flower Show at Corley Ash. The Knowles family organised the equestrian event and my father the sports. The miners were good athletes as well as very good customers in the bar!

Everyone was so poor after the Miner's Strike, which was followed by a General Strike, when men had no work and used to roam around the countryside begging for food. My father lost money due to the miners strike and business did not pick up again so we had to leave the pub. He could not find work so our family split up. I went to live with my father's mother in Birmingham and my sister Audrey and my mother went to live with her parents in Rugby. They were very hard days until my father found work and we could be together again.

Compiled from notes written by Joan Watts.

Outside Saracens Head. Fillongley & Corley Residents going on a day trip (1950c)
Names from top left. Names not in perfect order due to complexity of picture. Mother with child - Ward, Mother with child - Poole, (?), (?), Mrs Fowdry, Mrs. Dolby, Dougie Cashmore, (?), (?), Freddie Artin, Albert Courts, Brenda Nash, Arthur West, (?), (?), (?), Jim Phillips, ? Nelmes, ? Betteridge, Mrs. Davis, Jean Davis, Mrs. Burns, Des Hancox, Tony West, David Barrack, Johnny Cashmore, (?), Graham Hancox, (?), (?), (?), (?), (?), Betteridge, Mrs. Nash, Mrs Kenny, (?), Bob Scatttergood, Kitty ?, Thelma Cashmore, Mrs. Hancox, (?), (?), (?), Mrs. Courts, Betty West (girl with dark classes), Kath Beat West. Centre children: (?), (?), ? Nelmes, Freddie Hancox, Kate West, Barbara West, (?), Anne Brassington, Jimmy Burns, Maria Burns, (?), ? Betteridge, Peter Fowdry, Peter Poulett, Jill Barrack, Keith Haywood, (?), (?), (?), Lyn Westwood, (?), (?), (?), (?), (?), Man Kneeling with child - Tom Nash, Right- hand kneeling - Mr. Poulett, Jim Burns, Susan Catlow, (?), Ron Barrack. Photo from Barbara Magor (nee West) also - 1955 Brownie Pack and 1953 School.

Esna Balder *(nee Cooke)*

I was born in 1923 and I was taken to see the Headmaster, Mr. Bartlett, before I began school. I sat on a high stool while he asked me questions. I was to be in Mrs. Spencer's class. Each morning began with prayers, then a bible story then our times tables. We had lists of two and three letter words. We chanted these when Mrs. Spencer pointed at them. We learnt to write on slates. We had reading every day and stood in a circle following word for word while Mrs. Spencer walked round and round, keeping her eagle eye on us. She had two age groups to contend with. In the afternoon we rested on a straw mat.

Mrs. Spencer had a cupboard where she kept old shoes. Children who had walked a long distance in bad weather, could have their wet shoes and clothes dried on the hearth and fireguard and we would be in this wet steamy atmosphere all day. We took half a penny and she would make us a cup of cocoa. Mrs. Spencer had tremendous patience and a great sense of humour. At the age of seven we went into Miss Kay's room where we had proper desks, pens, ink and paper to write on.

When I was in the infants, I remember someone coming to measure children for the charity boots. Some mothers were given blankets and 'tailor Mathews' made skirts and trousers. We didn't think we were poor. We had plenty to eat, presents for birthdays and holidays with aunts and uncles. Many parents were lethargic in sending their children to school and they were threatened that Mr. Fell, the School Inspector would be after them! I had scarlet fever and was in the isolation hospital for about nine weeks.

Scarlet fever was a thing to be dreaded but diphtheria was worse and one girl I knew, Ida Lowe, died of it. The school nurse came round and looked at our heads. Some children had dirty heads and fleas. Some children had ringworm, which was treated with coal tar.

My father was a very intelligent man but he had not the education behind him. Mother had passed a scholarship to grammar school, but could not go. They both thought, that though we were girls, we should be educated. I passed to go to Nuneaton High School and a local charity paid my school fees and train fare. Mum and Dad paid for everything else. When my sister passed, she had to be paid for. Our parents made great sacrifices. Mother only had a new dress about every three years. Father had two jobs, down the pit and on the farm. The rest of the work my mother did on the smallholding. It was a hard life. We had no electricity, water was fetched from a well two fields away and rain water caught. Our weekly bath was on a Friday in the washhouse. We changed our underclothes once a week and our top clothes were washed when they were dirty. We were never uncomfortable and we were always well clothed. I left school at seventeen. I wanted to teach but decided to be a nurse. This was the one thing a girl could do with free training and I would become independent and ease the burden at home.

Compiled from oral recording (1992) See also her mother's memories (Kate Cooke) in Little Packington chapter.

Fillongley Brownie Pack (1955c)
Back Row: Esna Balder,
Kathleen Foulkes, Ruth ?, (?),
Pamela Wallbank, Lillian Palmer,
Lyn Westwood, Doreen Sprig,
Jean Balder, 'Nurse' Gardener.
Front Row: Christine Balder,
Ann Preece, Susan Hill,
Barbara West, Sandra Rider, (?), (?),
Corrie Brassington, (?).

Memories of Fillongley School

Francis Gordon Nightingale

I was born in 1925 at Fir Tree Farm, Wood End, Fillongley. The farm had about twenty-one acres. There was no electric then and we had candles and paraffin lamps that had to be pumped up. We had our water from a well in the yard and in the kitchen, Mother cooked on an old black range that used coal. We had no bathroom and we had a tin bath in front of the fire. We had three steam engines standing in the yard. When tractors came in, I imagine those steam engines went for scrap but I wish we had kept them.

I went to Fillongley School and Mrs. Spencer was the teacher and was lovely. Then there was Mr. Darling, who took the higher class and Mr. Whitaker, the headmaster. I only got caned once when I was acting about and throwing a dishcloth in the woodwork class. Mr. Whitaker was very strict.

I did not do any work on the farm before I left School. I had no brothers or sisters and played around with the rest of the boys, playing football and cricket. I remember Mr. Keatley, the blacksmith. We used to stand and watch him shoe the horses. When I left school I had no choice, I went straight to work on the farm. I was paid £2. 0s. 0d. a week by my father. I carried on the contracting business and now my sons are in charge. Things have changed now we have the chemical sprays and I think there is too much spraying done. We are always getting farmers ringing us to do the spraying. Both my sons, Alan and John, went to Fillongley School and my father, Alan and myself, were all taught by Mrs. Spencer.

Compiled from oral recording (1989)

Percy Nightingale ploughing

Haymaking and steam engine Thomas Nightingale? and farm hands at High House Farm.

Robert Seale

The Hubbard family (1914-15) outside Broomfield House, Wood End Lane
Standing: Ada Francis, (?), Ambrose, Ethel, Zillah. Seated: Mr. John Hubbard, Mrs. Mary Hubbard. Children: Elsie, Leonard and Ambrose Mander (cousin). Dog – Toby.

Maypole (1952c)
Boy right: Pete Warden. Notes: Children had to sit round the pole to stop it falling over. The horseshoe in blue bricks above the window, commemorate blacksmiths, Thomas and Jacob Hubbard, who had their smithy here until this room was built in 1921.

I was born at Curzon House, Fillongley in 1934. The house was rented from Les Cox, the village baker. When my father was killed in a motorbike accident in 1939, we went to live with my mother's father and brother (Hubbard) at Broomfield House in Wood End Lane. They rented Broomfield House from Mr. Kelsey. It was a big old house with two stairways. We were very poor, just scraping through. My mother used to do odd jobs and grandfather and my uncle used to help. We had chickens and grew most of our own vegetables. We did get a bit of help from the charities with new shoes and clothes. Most of the time, I had hob nailed boots because they lasted a long time and my uncle was always repairing them.

I started at Fillongley School when I was five and didn't like it when I first went. I kept trying to run home. Miss Morley was my first teacher, then Mrs. Spencer. Mrs. Spencer was the kindest teacher I ever had. The headmaster, Mr. Whittaker, was very strict and if things went wrong, he could be nasty but I didn't get the cane. The women teachers seemed to have more patience than the men. Beryl Owen from Wood End used to teach and play the piano. Mr. Darling was cantankerous. I think there must have been a shortage of teachers during the war years as Mr. Whittaker did a lot of teaching. I don't think I learnt a lot. I wasn't a very good learner and was more interested in playing sports, working on the farms with the horses and helping my grandfather. When school dinners came in, I didn't like them. They tried to make me eat cabbage and greens, although I was happy eating the puddings and jam tarts with custard on!

We had to go to Herbert Fowler in Arley to do woodwork each week. The Arley kids tried to be a bit rough with us but they were all right, once they got to know us. I stayed at Fillongley School until I was eleven and then went on to Herbert Fowler. I was given a 'council' bicycle to get to school and I was really happy to have my own bike. Herbert Fowler had better sports facilities and football. When my mother got married again, we moved away from the village to Honiley and I went to school at Balsall Common. It was quite a wrench to move away but I found Balsall Common School a happier school and the children friendlier.

Compiled from interview (2000)

Graham Spencer

THE COVENTRY BLITZ

I spent my early childhood at Slowly Hall Farm, near Daw Mill and moved to Fillongley in 1939, when I was six. The day war was declared, my grandmother taped up all the cracks around the doors and windows in case of a gas attack. We lived at Curzon House and had evacuees come to stay with us. My father was a chauffeur but during the war he worked in a munitions factory. The night of the Coventry Blitz, my father should have come home by 8pm. My mother stood at the bottom of the drive and waited for him. We could hear the bombing and saw that Coventry was ablaze. The next morning we all waited anxiously. He came back at 12 noon and told us how horrendous it had been.

I was in Mrs. Spencer's class when I started at Fillongley School. She was a very nice lady, gentle and patient. The headmaster, Jack Whittaker, was a tyrant. He didn't hit me but he was very fond of the cane and he also cuffed boys round the ears. He tried to teach good habits. He played the piano with one finger and if we didn't get the hymns right, we had to stay in after school. Each morning, three of us fetched meat and vegetables so they could make the school dinners. We fetched meat from Mr. Gilbert, the butcher, and vegetables from Mr. Foster at the Post Office. When we were eleven or twelve, we had to light the fires for the ovens. The toilets were outside the school and they were a disgrace. Buckets that were never cleaned.

We had a good education at Fillongley but I failed the eleven-plus. We were not coached to take exams. It was quite a culture shock when I went to Herbert Fowler. The school had far better facilities, a science room with Bunsen burners and a gym. Classes were more varied and they had some very good teachers.

Compiled from oral recording (2002)

Fillongley School (1930's)
Back Row: Joe Glover, Frank West, Alf Wagstaff, Bill Wood, Eric Jones, Frank Keatley, George Watkins, Alf Keatley, Arthur Brereton.
Centre Row: Rev. Waldigrave, Thelma Fox, Mary Fulford, Annie Brereton, Hetty Atkins, Gwen Lawrence, Doris Shaw, Freda Paice,
Headmaster - Mr. Bartlett. Front Row: (?), Joe Matthews, Eric Taylor, Bert Tandy.

Fillongley Village (1915c)
Photographer: Sidwell, Meriden. Mr. Coton with his horse was the last 'carrier' in Fillongley. (See extract in Mrs. Spencer's memories).

Girls Friendly Society, Morris Dancers (1913)

Back row: Mary Ledbrook, Mabel Coles, Lizzie Arthurs, Francis Gerrard-Dinn, Rhoda Gerrard-Dinn, Annie Arthurs, Dorothy Ibbotson, Bertha Taylor, Betty Bishop, Chrissie Bennett. Front row: Gladys Lancaster, Francis Scattergood, Bessie Matthews, Edith Ibbotson, Sybil Boswell, Ruth Ledbrook, Ethel Clark, Doris Boswell.

Fillongley Infant School (1953)

Back Row: Keith Haywood, Victor Anderton, Roy Smith, (?), Miss Freeman. Centre Row: Edith Currier, Lesley Shakespear, Jane Cooper, Christine Green, Margaret Foulkes, Margaret Woodward, Alan Brassington, Jeffrey Ridgley, Heather Platt, (?), Lyn Westwood, Denise Reybold, Pauline Riddel. Front Row: Peter Wolf, Jimmy Knapp, Hilma McClure, Ann Kelsey, Doreen Sprig, Ruth Wood, Susan Hill, Rita Reading, June Beard, Barbara West, Brenda Andrews, Graham Williams, ? Matthews.

Memories of Fillongley School

CHAPTER SIX

Little Packington School and house (1999) View from footbridge

LITTLE PACKINGTON SCHOOL

Great Packington and Little Packington are mainly connected to the Packington Estate, owned by the Earl of Aylesford. They are not 'true' villages, but scattered farms and cottages with a rectory and small church on the Great Packington Estate. In 1841, Great Packington had 60 houses and 340 inhabitants and Little Packington, 29 houses and 151 inhabitants. Most were employed working on the estate or in the great house - Packington Hall. Little Packington School is also known as the Earl of Aylesford's School and is next to the ford on the River Blythe, about three and a half miles south of Coleshill. Although in a picturesque location, one wonders why they built a school next to a river that frequently floods? The only charity to provide for schooling was set up in 1788, when Rev. James Jackques left £6.0s 0d per annum for a schoolmistress to teach ten poor children to read and say the catechism in the Church. The school closed in 1955 and can be seen from the ford, in derelict condition, behind the schoolhouse that is still occupied.

THE CASTLE FAMILY - TEACHERS 1905 - 1915

In 1905, a schoolmaster was required for Little Packington School. The minutes of the School Manager's meeting record that they discussed that the cheapest option would be to employ a husband and wife with a grown up daughter who could teach. The two females would supervise the girls and could also act as mandatory chaperones when the pupil teachers were receiving after-hours' instruction.

The position of Head Master was advertised in the 'School Master Magazine'. Mr. Ernest Castle applied and was appointed from seventy applicants from all over the country. He left his home in Ringsfield, Surrey, with his wife Grace and four children, Annie, Don, Arthur and Madge. Their daughter, Amy, stayed as a teacher in Suffolk. Had he been aware, in advance, of the damp conditions of the school and how it would affect his family, he may not have taken up the position.

Ernest Castle was eleven when he started teaching, probably as a pupil teacher before taking his exams. He signed himself as a 1st Class Certificated Teacher. He had twelve children and his two sons both obtained scholarships to go to Coleshill Grammar School. Madge was five when they arrived and her sister Annie was aged twenty-three and taught in the school alongside her Father. Mrs Castle taught the infants until 1907, when due to ill health, she had to give up teaching. Annie took her place and taught the infants until 1915. Father and daughter did not see 'eye to eye' and his entries in the School Log Book make a point of noting whenever she was late or absent from duty.

Arthur's health suffered due to the damp conditions of the schoolhouse. He underwent an operation in 1906 on his tonsils and adenoids. Dr. Wall, assisted by a colleague, performed the operation on the kitchen table. Madge remembered how the doctor's hand slipped and more of Arthur's throat than was advisable was removed. He never properly regained his health and died in 1918.

ILLNESS

As with all the village schools, children suffered from various illnesses. If children could not attend, their names were removed from the school register. Alfred William - consumption. Harry Wells - consumption. Annie Maidment - delicate health. William Wall - has an operation on his side. Sidney Moseley - suffering from diseased kidneys. Lizzie Smith - Birmingham General Hospital where she died from complications after an appendectomy and two further operations. Canon Waller and his daughter both took a keen interest in the school. Canon Waller was responsible for visiting the school weekly, verifying the registers and liaising with the Board of School Managers. He also took Scripture lessons. His daughter, Marion Waller, was a School Manager and visited the school to join in hymn singing, inspect the sewing and bring presents and organise tea for the pupils. Canon Waller died in 1910 and Marion in 1911. Colonel J.H. Monckton took over his duties and the Rev. W.J. Locke and his wife visited occasionally, distributed prizes and ran the Penny Bank. A.J. Sidwell was the School Attendance Officer. Mr. Ernest Castle retired from teaching in 1915 after fifty-four years of service.

Compiled from a booklet written by Angela Raby (granddaughter of Ernest Castle). Copies of the book on Little Packington School and the Castle family are at Warwick Record Office and Coleshill Museum. Log Books at Warwick Record Office.

SCHOOL INSPECTOR'S REPORTS

In 1910, the report by the School Inspector, Mr. E.H. Carter, described the children as quiet and orderly…. "but in order to make teaching thoroughly effective it will be necessary to adopt methods which will develop more self reliance and stimulate more active individual effort." He goes on to say that "only a vague knowledge has been gained so far in Geography and History." He was also concerned about the large, unsuitable desks in the classroom as "they take up too much floor space and insufficient room is left for games and physical movement." The floor of the classroom was only washed once a year and he recommended arrangements be made for frequent washing of the floor forthwith!

Mr. Castle was in his sixties and probably set in his ways, but he did make a token effort to improve the teaching by reducing the drawing and needlework lessons and to have more essay lessons and botany. One year later, in March 1911, Mr. Carter visited the school again, however his main concern this time was not the teaching methods but the condition of the school!

Premises:
1. The building as a school is built on the banks of a river, which overflows when there are heavy rains. When this happens, the School premises and house become inundated, and the water gets through the gratings under the floor. The resulting dampness has affected the health of two of the teachers.
2. The School was closed ten times this school year on account of the floods.
3. Some of the children have to cross over a bridge near the School and the supports of the bridge are dilapidated. The path from and to it are sometimes flooded and impassable.
4. Boys cloakroom not ventilated. The girls cloakroom is very small and not ventilated.
5. There is no proper washing apparatus for the children.
6. Each of the boys and girls closets should have its own door, so that it may be quite private in accordance with the Building Regulations.
7. Both rooms are very narrow. It is very difficult to ventilate properly the Infants room, which has no apex ventilation.

(During the floods of 1916, the central sections of the bridge were swept away.)

Ernest and Grace Castle family (1895)
Standing: Amy, Annie. Sitting: Claude, Cyril, Mrs. Castle with Don, Mr. Castle with Arthur.

Kate Cooke (nee Horsely)

I WOULD CRY TO GO TO SCHOOL

I was born in a little thatched cottage at Moat Farm, Little Packington in 1900. Mother would milk the cows of a morning and I would take the milk to Packington Hall and deliver it around the lodge keepers, gardeners and coachman and then go to school for nine o'clock. The school was near the ford and I was three years old when I began. I would cry because everyone else was at school so Mr. Castle said I could go to school from 11am until lunchtime. Miss Castle was the infant teacher and Mr. Castle the head. We had slates and slate pencils to begin with. We did have books and we learnt reading, writing, arithmetic, spelling, geography, history, needlework, crotchet and knitting. We had a good all round education. The Canon and Miss Waller would organise Christmas concerts and in summer we would go to the Rectory for parties. Miss Waller would visit everyone - a lovely family. She came into the school every Monday morning and we would practice the psalms. We had to go to Church three times on a Sunday. We were all in the choir, father as well.

The School Inspector made regular visits to the school. There were between fifty and sixty children in the school. They were big families, most in agriculture. We wore ordinary clothes to school with a white pinafore to protect our dresses. We only had a new dress perhaps twice a year. Boys wore dresses until they were two or three. We played hopscotch and skipping, but I liked reading best.

We would drive the cows down to the river of an evening to graze for about an hour. We had two fields and two meadows on the other side of the river that we cut for hay. We would stand on the bridge and watch the cars go through the ford. If they got stuck we would go and get Mr. Rigby and his horse to pull them out. We got 3d for that.

I was in Upper Grade IV for two years but they would not let me leave school until I was fourteen. It was difficult to get any further education, as you had to get from Little Packington to Hampton Station then on to Warwick. There were nine servants at Packington Hall and I started working in the kitchen, making the toast, before I left school. When my parents went to school, they paid a penny a week and took their own slate and pencil. Father went to school at Kineton and my mother at Catherine-de-Barnes.

Compiled from oral recording. See also her daughter's memories, Esna Balder in Fillongley chapter.
Further extract on Kate Cooke in book, 'I remember Strawberries and Sewage.'

Little Packington School (pre 1920) Headmaster Mr. Comber?

Joyce Benson (nee Dutton)

THREAT OF SCHOOL CLOSURE

I started school at the beginning of the 1920's, at the age of three and a half. The reason for this early start was the threat of the school closing for lack of pupils, so closing country schools down is not a new idea. Mr. Comber was the headmaster and after he left, Mrs. Morris came as headmistress. Her husband had been gassed in the war, so was unable to work. He did the cooking and housework for her. They had a young daughter called Cicily. A friend of theirs, Miss Thompson came with them as infant teacher. I think they came from Lancashire. Mr. Morris used to fatten-up geese for Christmas. If they got out of the garden, they used to chase us. Many times we were stuck in the school toilets, which were outside, too scared to come out and face the geese.

During the winter, we had days off because of the river being in flood and the school was surrounded by water. Sometimes we had to hurry and leave school early if the river began to rise. At Christmas, we had a lovely party with a large tree supplied by Lord Aylesford and a very good present off the tree.

Each morning, Mrs. Morris used to read interesting things out of the newspaper, which came by post, so we were well informed in what was happening in the country. Miss Thompson left and we had a new teacher. She used to take some of us girls for lunchtime walks in Packington Park. We usually met a young gamekeeper and she stopped for a chat. Was this the reason for the walks?

When I was four years old, my family moved to Great Packington and I had to walk, with my brother who was eight, over three miles to school. At the age of twelve, we moved once again, this time to Meriden. I am sure we received a good education at Packington School. We could read, write and certainly didn't need calculators to add up.

By the ford is a small island with stepping-stones. During the summer in the lunch break, we used to cross over to the island to eat our sandwiches, swing on the trees and play hide and seek. The school and school house was built in the shape of an L with three rooms. The large schoolroom had a wooden stage at one end, a large open fire surrounded by a guard. In the winter, a kettle was boiled on the fire to make cocoa. We took cocoa and sugar mixed together in a tin and milk in a bottle. The middle room was called the 'library' and it was full of old books but I don't remember reading any of them.

The third room was the infant's classroom. This was where the schoolhouse was joined on. One of the bedrooms was over this classroom. The classrooms were very light because they had many windows high up, so we couldn't see through them unless you stood on the desks. They were certainly happy times I spent at Little Packington School.

Compiled from notes written by Joyce Benson.

Little Packington School (1924c)
Standing: Miss Thompson, Mrs. Morris. Back Row: Stanley Shuttleworth, Bill Stanley, George Hall, Jack Dutton. 3rd Row: Doug Dyer, Robert Moseley, Joyce Dutton, Joan Stanley, (?), ? Bartholomew, Jack Dyer. 2nd Row: ? Bartholomew, Rebecca Boyson, Nellie Dyer, Vera Arrell, Nelly Roberts, Aprila Bartholomew, Elsie Mosley, ? Dyer. Front Row: Winnie Roberts, Pat Page, Cicely Morris, Mary Page, Nellie Roberts.

John Wall

My family came from Great Packington. I was fifth generation and we lived in the Thatched Cottage (burnt down 1986). I suppose my ancestors had worked on the estate but my father worked for Warwickshire County Council. I was five when I started school. I cycled to school along a track through the estate on a hand-made bike, which was a frame and two wheels. The school had no electricity and was very old fashioned. Oil lamps hung swinging from the ceiling. In the winter the river used to rise and cut the school off for several days at a time. The children came from three different directions, Little Packington, Great Packington and down the lane. We would get to the waters edge and our teacher, Mrs. Fountain, would come into the garden and call out the register. Then we would all go home again – chuffed!

School dinners came in metal containers from the Coleshill side and the driver would unload the containers onto the bridge and we children would have to fetch them in. We didn't have bottled milk. We had fresh milk we used to fetch in a bucket from Mr. Barber's farm across the river. We used to go for nature walks, and this was when the trains were still running. I got the biggest telling off of my life for being on the wrong side of the track when a train came through.

The School house (1999)

The school was dying. It wasn't like a school regime. There just weren't enough children. There were eight pupils when it closed in 1955. I was seven years old and I was sent to Meriden School.

Compiled from oral recording (1996)
Further extract in Meriden Chapter.

The Ford at Little Packington with the School behind (1999)
(Author's note: The Ford is a popular (but scruffy) picnic spot, where I have often come on warm summer days.
Foreground: my daughter Andrea with her children Emma, and Clara in the boat.)

Trixie (Beatrice) Postings *(nee Dolphin)*

WILD VIOLETS

I was born in Maxstoke, in 1912, in a little cottage that has since been demolished. There were fields and lots of wild flowers and I loved the violets growing wild in the banks. A family who lived down the lane had a baby who died; one of my earliest memories is of him, laid in the coffin with a small bunch of wild violets in his hand.

I was chosen as May Queen one year. We went round the village to collect flowers and made garlands and afterwards we had a tea party. I think the reason I was voted May Queen was because my two elder brothers bullied all the kids to vote for me. At the end of the party they had three cheers for different people and they all said 'three cheers' for my mother. I ran home to tell my Mum she was going to have three new chairs!

MAXSTOKE AND LITTLE PACKINGTON SCHOOLS

I don't remember much about the education at Maxstoke but I do remember that I learnt to knit socks in white cotton on four pins, and was very pleased when I could turn a heel. Miss Cottrill was head teacher and she was also my God Mother and Miss Haden was the infant's teacher.

Next I went to Little Packington as my father went to work for Lord Aylesford on the Packington Estate. I have no recollection of that school, except that there was a Christmas concert and I was Fairy Light O'Gold and my brother was Man in the Moon. I had a wand and tinsel and I thought it was wonderful.

Compiled form oral recording (1996)
Further extract in Meriden Chapter.

Maxstoke School Sports Day (1950-60's)
Left to right: Miss Graveson, Joan Cartwright, Jackie Waite and Jane Cooper, June Rollason, Bertha Rollason, Stella Fetherstone-Dilke, Mary Gold, Pauline Fetherstone-Dilke, Dora Lake, Ruth Green, Mrs. Wharton, Mrs. Beresford, Rosemarie Beresford, Mildred Jones, Maureen Jones, Joyce Knight.

CHAPTER SEVEN

Maxstoke School (1909)

MAXSTOKE C. OF E. SCHOOL

On the northern boundary of Fillongley is the tiny village of Maxstoke, typical of a scattered settlement in the old forest of Arden with the lovely river Blythe meandering through to Coleshill, about three miles away. Maxstoke has an air of mystery with a ruined priory close to the church (which was probably constructed from its ruins) and a picturesque moated castle, once the seat of the Clintons and now owned by the Featherstone-Dilkes. In 1850, there were about 68 houses, 346 inhabitants, a tailor, shopkeeper, blacksmith, shoemaker and the Three Horse Shoes public house. An average of sixty children attended school and John and Maria Etchells were the master and mistress. Today there are no shops, pub or village school.

In most villages, the school is situated close to the Church but in Maxstoke, it is about one-mile away. I discovered from local residents that there had been a 'school' next to the church in an open barn and then it was held in an upstairs room of a house, opposite the Church. The school was erected in 1845, supported by voluntary contributions and was called 'Maxstoke Endowed School.' It changed to a Church of England School and was enlarged, probably around 1913. It was always a 'happy' school and did not suffer from overcrowding. The children had time off to celebrate various events and had the added benefit of treats at the castle and vicarage. As with most Church schools, it was under funded and the provision of materials and books were inadequate. For boys, who were not interested in knitting or sewing, there were times when the education left something to be desired! Later it changed to a council school and sadly, was closed in 1967, due to insufficient numbers.

MAXSTOKE SCHOOL LOG BOOKS

The first entries of the Maxstoke School Log Book were made by Mrs. Hutchins, the head teacher, who may have been the vicar's wife. She had a constant struggle to keep the school open with high absenteeism. The school was financed on the number of children who regularly attended and teachers tried various ways (and threats) to get children to attend. This was difficult as country children, boys in particular, were unruly and undisciplined. Children were expected to help with haymaking, harvests, to pick cowslips, blackberries, acorns, potatoes or wild flowers. During November and December, when the local gentry had their game shoots, children stayed off school to go 'beating' in the woods. The teacher had little or no say in these matters as farmers and local gentry were also the school governors! Added to this, various infectious diseases and bad weather also kept children away. The School Inspector, however, would not have accepted these as good reasons for the low academic standards!

EXTRACTS FROM MAXSTOKE SCHOOL LOG BOOKS

Mrs. Hutchins entered for duty. Few present owing to weather

8th Jan	1867	Rev. Hutchins visited bringing inks, pens etc.
18th Jan	1867	Clara Bentley cautioned for fighting.
1st Mar	1867	James Rix withdrawn to work at the mill.
11th Aug	1871	Several absent – in harvest fields.
9th Oct	1871	Attendance better – fines commenced.
31st Oct	1871	Several absent – acorning.
7th Nov	1871	First class given lessons on paper!
25th Feb	1873	No school – deep snow.
10th May	1873	Several absent - picking cowslips.
20th Oct	1873	W. Bolus gone to work at the castle.
11th Dec	1878	Jane Torbitt gone to Work House.
7th Apr	1879	W. Johnson at home to gather wild flowers.
21st Apr	1879	James Smith left – gone to America.

Gatehouse, Maxstoke Priory (1999)

GRANTS FOR YEAR :   1879 - £34. 7s 0d. (Attendance 40). 1880 - £31. 3s. 0d. 1881 - £29. 14s. 0d.

7th Nov	1884	School closed – outbreak of diphtheria.
19th Nov	1884	The well is opened and cleaned by order of the Doctor.
9th May	1887	Children invited to compete for the Jubilee medals offered by the Sheriff of Warwickshire.
21st June	1887	Jubilee. Major Dilke presented children with a mug, plate and portrait of Queen Victoria.
16th Dec	1887	Many boys absent - gone beating in the woods.
9th Feb	1888	First lesson - on addition of money.
1st May	1888	Holiday - May treat.
10th May	1888	Ascension Day. Small school, many children stayed away to attend Church.
5th May	1893	Several away with whooping cough.
29th May	1893	The Gold children away with scarlet fever.
6th Nov	1893	The Fallon children away with scarlet fever.
12th Dec	1893	An Order to close the school until new year because of fever.
4th Feb	1895	Attendance fair - deep snow. New harmonium has come for the school.
8th Feb	1895	Cold most intense, only 9 at school. Lesson on metals and coins.
2nd May	1895	Many away attending the funeral of Nellie Cross.
27th Sept	1895	Several away this week gathering fruit.
8th Jan	1897	Commenced system of weekly attendance tickets
17th Jan	1897	Two boys absent with ringworm.
22nd June	1897	Holiday for Queen Victoria's Diamond Jubilee Treat.
14th Jan	1898	37 children in school. Very satisfactory.
14th May	1898	Charles Gold left, gained scholarship to Coleshill Grammar School.
31st May	1900	Half holiday - 'Surrender of Pretoria.'
20th July	1900	Half-day holiday in honour of the School Inspector's visit.
30th July	1900	Birmingham School Board visited to see the working of a rural school.
28th Jan.	1901	A Memorial Service in Church on Saturday, on the occasion of the Queen's funeral.
30th Aug	1901	Skin eruptions on the face of one pupil.
1st Oct	1901	Parents advised to keep some pupils away. Alarmed at the development of skin eruptions.
1st Dec	1901	Daisy Lyndon unable to attend all week for lack of good shoes.
12th May	1902	Mina Ford absent - aggravated form of ringworm.
25th–30th June	1902	School closed on account of village rejoicings to celebrate the King's coronation.
7th July	1902	*Inspector's Report. 'Spoken and written answers of children of this small school give evidence of much careful and conscientious work on the part of the teachers.'*
23rd Jan	1903	Harry Woodfield absent all week to wait upon a sick grandmother.
4th Sept	1903	Poor attendance in a.m. - Coleshill Horse Show.
26th July	1905	Half-day holiday - Annual Tea Party at Vicarage.

3rd Dec	1905	Miss Back brought plans and charts on Whitacre, 'Coventry Municipal Water Supply.'
18th Oct	1909	Brook's family returned. Away 2 days for the purpose of cleansing their clothes and bodies.
14th May	1913	Attendance Officer visited. Dispatched mentally deficient children resident in this parish.
22nd May	1913	Empire Day observed by lessons on the Empire.
7th Sept	1913	Examination of heads by Health Visitor. Warnings given to several with verminous heads.
19th Feb	1916	Telegram from Warwick. School closure 20th Feb - 1st March. Whooping cough epidemic.
28th Mar	1916	Top classes attended lecture on 'Food for Fitness.'
26th Mar	1917	Mrs. Hemmings visited regarding case of 'cow pox' in family.
15th June	1917	Ivy Mansell kept away 5 weeks to mind baby while her mother is employed in fieldwork.
10th Aug	1917	W. Bagley employed all the week. W. Tolley and S. Dolphin both employed for part week.
12th Sept	1918	Medical Certificate received. Lillie Parker suffering from tuberculosis.
12th Nov	1918	Holiday to celebrate the signing of the Armistice and Service of Thanksgiving.
16th Oct	1924	Doctor visited to vaccinate five children against smallpox.
1st May	1923	Frances Hollyoak began duties as headmistress. Miss Edkins as supplementary teacher.
29th May	1923	Received stock, exercise books, white calico handkerchiefs.
9th Feb	1926	School closed. Children taken to pantomime in Birmingham.
11th Feb	1926	Discussion by Managers on means of raising money for the new school piano.
23rd July	1926	Children left at 3.30pm for school treat at Maxstoke Castle by Mrs. Dilke.

20th June   1928   *School Inspector's Report.*

'There are some good features in this school, one of the best being the tidiness and good handwriting shown … otherwise it is impossible to regard progress in the fundamental subjects as satisfactory. Arithmetic is definitely weak and the older children failed in an easy test. Speech is uncouth and although the children can read their books in some fashion, they can give little account of the meaning of them. The truth is that the children will not do justice to their head mistress (who has the kindliest intentions towards them) until they are made to take more interest and put more effort in their work. In particular, the older boys are too casual in their attitude. They behave badly in the playground and the adjoining road.

31st Aug	1928	Frances Hollyoak resigned her appointment as Head Mistress. (See her memories.)
25th Apr	1933	Harold and Steve Hartop excluded for 3 weeks suffering from Chicken Pox.
22nd May	1933	Orderly arrangement for mid-day meal commenced.
15th June	1934	During past week school has been carried out in the Open Air.
5th July	1934	School closed for the day for Seaside Outing to Llandudno.
25th Sept	1936	Milk supplied to 24 children under the "Milk in Schools" scheme.
4th Sept	1939	Re-opened after Summer vacation. Owing to War, unofficially opened - only 8 attended.
5th Sept	1939	School again opened only 2 attended. Opened every morning for week - no children attended.
2nd Feb	1940	No children attended all the week – all roads practically impassable.
23rd July	1940	H.M. Inspector visited re: Savings Groups. Talked to children on 'Importance of Saving.'
30th Aug	1940	Attendance not as good this week owing to frequent Air Raids.
12th Sept	1940	Scarlet Fever in Beresford family so therefore absent.
12th May	1941	Doctor and Nurse visited the school to carry out first stage of immunisation against Diphtheria
20th June	1941	Owing to bad air raid (many bombs dropped in village - no-one hurt) 20 attended only.
7th May	1945	Victory declared. School closed for celebrations 8th – 9th May.
12th June	1950	BBC came to listen to a World History programme with the children.
12th July	1950	School closed all day. Sunday School outing to Wicksteed Park.

Research by Nancy Bates.
Log books at Warwick Record Office.

Maxstoke Castle (2002)

Frances Woodfield *(nee Hollyoak)*

I was born in 1899, at High House Farm, Broad lane, Fillongley, the youngest of six and we went to Fillongley School. Harry Fletcher and my brother used to push me to school in a mail car, two miles there and two miles back. Mr. Kay was head master and he gave me piano lessons. Miss Peake used to teach me and she was always cross. My brother Sid and I both liked music and we used to go to Fillongley Church to practice on the organ.

One of my jobs as a child was to walk the Shire horses to Maxstoke to be shoed. The road then was a sandy track through the woods and I had to pass a big gypsy encampment near Maxstoke. My father would say I'd be all right, but I was afraid of the gypsies.

I passed to go to Nuneaton High. I had to pass an exam to be a pupil teacher and after five years I took another exam and went to college in Birmingham. I became a pupil teacher at Herbert Fowler, Arley. Two days a week I had to go to Nuneaton and meet in a house with other pupil teachers to be taught extra lessons. When I finished my training, I taught music in Coventry.

HEADMISTRESS OF MAXSTOKE SCHOOL

Several people in Maxstoke told me they were going to have a new headmistress. I thought it was just what I would love to do, but I thought I was too young as I was only twenty-three. I went to the vicar and put an application in. Four candidates came for the position but to my surprise, I was the one that was called back. My parents moved with me to Maxstoke as there was a big schoolhouse. The children had been left to go their own way for so many years and the reading books were terrible. Some of the children were most unruly and I had to give them the cane. Most of them were farmer's children. They were big strapping boys but I wore them down. I had to be tough or give up. I got new books, new desks and a new piano. The assistant teacher, Miss Edkins, introduced me to my husband and I left to be married in 1928, after being headmistress for five years. They had said to me when I came to the school, that I could play the Church organ any time I wanted to. I carried on playing as organist in Maxstoke Church for over fifty years.

Extract from oral recording made by Bill Bolton and Bernard Tranter (1980)

Frances Hollyoak, with her father (1923)

Maxstoke School (1929-30c)
Back row: Len Basketfield, Len Wallis, Stan Smith, Ernie Stevens. 4th row: Mrs. Haden, Cliff Herman, Reg Lewis, Jack Ellard, Ernest Jones, Tom Smith, George Ellard, Sid Stanley, Miss Edkins. 3rd row: Don Smith, Peggy Climer, Betty Climer, Jessica Stanley, Edith Stevens, Lillian Sanders, Dora Nash, Barbara Masters, Francis Masters, Olwyn Jones. 2nd Row: ? Saunders, Joe Wallis, (?), Dot Ellard, ? Mansell, Hazel Rollason, Daisy Baker, Joy Climer, ? Mansell, (?). Front Row: Tom Stanley, Jim Baker, Ted Baker, Jeff Basketfield, Phil Rollason, Sid Lewis, Bill Hartop, 'Bub' Basketfield.

Albert Sidney Dolphin

I was born in 1907 near Redditch and moved to a small cottage at Hall End in Maxstoke when I was two. My father worked on a farm with the animals, and like most families, we were poor. I had a brother and sister, Gilbert and Trixie. We had to fetch water from a spring by the stream and it took ages to fill a bucket. The washing-up was done outside as there was no room in the cottage. We had a bucket toilet that had to be emptied by digging a hole in the garden. My mother cooked on an open fire that heated an oven by the side. We had candles and paraffin lamps. One family we knew was so poor, they had a tea chest as a table, orange boxes as chairs and jam jars to drink from. If you had no food, there were no handouts and you had to go to Meriden Work House. One old person refused to go to the Work House and he went to stay in another person's cottage. They had to carry him out.

I started school when I was five and walked with Roland Smith. Miss Lillian Haden was the infant's teacher and we had slates to write on. Miss Cottrill was our next teacher and we had pen and inks. We learnt our times tables and we sometimes played card games where we had to guess the names of towns. The teacher read books to us and we did sums. They taught us quite well. There were about sixty children in the school. I remember getting the cane once. Not many children got the cane. On May Day we went round the village with flower garlands and on Empire Day we had a party across the road in a field at Mr. Graveson's farm. The children's nurse used to come and look for nits in our hair, and most children had them. She didn't do much except use a fine toothcomb to try and get them out. We learnt to grow vegetables in the headmistress's garden and some one stuck a fork in my foot!

Sidney, Gilbert, Mrs. Ellen Dolphin

Most children lived on farms and we looked forward to helping with the harvest on summer evenings. One or two farmers had fifty or sixty boys from Shawbury School to help clear the fields and single out mangels and swedes. It was at Shawbury School that I first saw the 'pictures,' a film of cowboys. We were not allowed to mix with Shawbury boys as they were considered 'naughty' boys but we were very friendly with the gypsies. They used to make pegs and help on the farms. They camped at the top end of Maxstoke we called the 'Back and Alice,' by Hall Farm. The gypsy children didn't go to school.

We swam in the river at Duke Bridge. One of the farmers used to dip his sheep in the river and there was a walk by the railway line to Little Packington. I would often collect moorhen eggs and I've eaten hundreds in my time. One day I fell into the river with my school uniform on. I had to wait hours for it to dry before I dare go home. We had no pocket money, so when people used to come through the village from Birmingham, in a sort of high carriage driven by four horses, we children ran after them and called out for a penny. We collected quite a lot of pennies but we had no shops to spend them! The man from the co-op used to call for the grocery order and they would deliver it later.

One day I was following the foxhounds with a friend. When we felt hungry, we found a field of swedes and we ate one each. Later, I didn't feel well. I had a pair of thatching pegs and had them under each arm to help me along. Lots of people had flu. I was ill for a long time, almost at death's door and my parents were also ill. When people died, the village bier went round and trundled through the village to the church with bearers - men you knew.

COLESHILL GRAMMAR SCHOOL

I went to Coleshill Grammar School when I was twelve. I didn't pass an exam but my parents paid for me to go. I think it was about £4. per term. It was quite different. The Rev. Somerset Bateman was head and he often thrashed pupils but never me. We got a very good education. I got the prize for arithmetic and science in my first year, so the education must have been good at Maxstoke. Billy Bagley lived up the lane from me and he also went to Coleshill. He used to keep a cuckoo in a cage. When I was older, we moved to Pickford Brook near Allesley. My brother and sister went to Meriden School and I had to cycle all the way to Coleshill.

Compiled from oral recording (1996)

Steve Hartop

I was born in 1926. My family had lived for four or five generations in Maxstoke, working in farming. My father worked in Coventry for Rover Motors and then went on to form his own business in Maxstoke. He married my mother, a local girl, Fanny Rollason. When we were young, my grandmother, who lived at Fir Tree Farm, would take me for walks in my pram while, at the same time, walking a cow along with us so that it could graze along the verges.

I was five when I started at Maxstoke School. In the afternoons we were put into deck chairs and told to go to sleep. The flush toilets, washbasins and tarmac playground were installed after the war but we had to make do with bucket toilets and wash our hands at the outside pump. I remember going on a school outing to Llandudno one year and Rhyl on another occasion. We were taken to Whitacre Station on a coal lorry where we caught the train. When we got there, we were as black as ink. We had summer parties at Maxstoke Castle and received a small present to take home. The field next to the school was full of cowslips and burnet in the summer time. We would pick the blooms and take them home for mother to make wine. I remember that we could have a week off school for potato picking. I don't remember being paid but we were given potatoes to take home.

Our head mistress, Mrs. Haden, was fond of knitting and if she had a complicated pattern, we were asked to do quiet reading. We were all very good at reading by the time we left her school! She also taught a lot of geography, but mathematics was hopeless. At eleven years of age I was still trying to work out what a decimal point was. I was never really bored as there were glorious playtimes, trees to climb and fields to play in and we were always sloping off to help (or annoy) local farmers. We didn't have a good schooling, but the cane was never used and I left Maxstoke with a thirst for education.

At eleven I went to Coleshill School where they had split leather straps to hit you. The strap came round the back and front of the hand as well. I used to get it frequently! You had two strokes for talking, four for being cheeky and twelve for truant.

Compiled from interview (1996) and notes written by Steve Hartop.

Sylvia Hartop (nee Waldram)

I moved to Maxstoke from Curdworth in 1954 when I married my husband, Steve. We spent two years prior to our marriage, renovating the thatched cottage that Brigham Young, one of the founder members of the Mormon Church, had lived in between 1839-41. Shortly after my marriage, there was a vacancy for an infant teacher at Maxstoke School and I was fortunate to spend the next four years working with her. Previously, Miss Mary Graveson had been the infant teacher, but had left to spend some time in Australia. Coincidentally, as I left, she returned and took up the post again.

Mrs. Bowden, like many of her generation of teachers, was totally dedicated to the development of each child who passed through her school. She taught every part of the curriculum with remarkable success. No child would be moved up to the next class unless fully ready to do so, which never took more than an extra week or two. Good behaviour was the norm. Respect and kindness to other teachers and fellow pupils was the expectation within the school. This was achieved by the kindness and respect shown by Mrs. Bowden, herself, to her pupils and staff. Mrs. Bowden and Miss Graveson, organised the 1951 historical pageant, which involved most of the village and was talked about for years afterwards. At Christmas time, special attention was given to our school plays and afterwards, tea would be served to parents and other visitors. In the summer, we would go for nature walks. On Wednesdays, Wright's grocery van would call and the children were allowed to spend their pocket money, on sweets or fruit, which Mrs. Bowden saw as 'educational.'

A high number of pupils went on to the grammar schools, but all of the pupils were fully prepared for their senior education. Having lived in the village for so long, I have had the opportunity to see the results of Mildred Bowden's work, which is impressive.

Compiled from interview and notes written by Sylvia Hartop.

Charles Woodfield

I was born in Lambeth, London in 1925. My mother was a domestic servant in Dorset and my father is unknown. I was fostered in North Wolds, Peterborough with Mr. and Mrs. Cuthbert and their son, until I was six. They were kind and good to me. Then I remember they put a pink ticket on me and I was sent on a train, in the guards van, to Snowshill Station, Birmingham. I was met by the Master of the Church of England Children's Home. I cried my eyes out, as no one had explained where I was going and I didn't understand what was happening to me.

The Children's Home was very strict. There were thirty or more children in a big house in Moseley. Most boys got hit, it was the only way they knew of quieting them. The odd one escaped and when they were brought back, they were in trouble! They did teach you to work. There was always a job to do. You had to do as you were told and if you didn't eat your meal one day, you had it the next day. We were always inspected before we went to school.

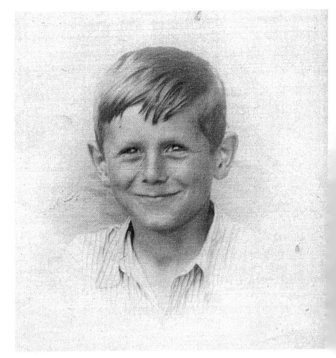

Charles Woodfield

ADOPTED

My 'parents' came and picked me out when I was ten; they said they chose me because I was small and the others were 'bully heads.' I don't remember other people coming but some of the children were sent off to Canada and Australia. A master from the Home took me to Washwood on the train and we met the Coleshill vicar who brought me to Maxstoke and my new home. No one explained anything to me and I when I got there, I sat crying my eyes out in front of the fire and the cat came and sat on me.

My new 'mother' was strict and she ruled everyone. Their children had grown up and away. That's why they had me, so I could work. She was the oldest one of ten and everyone was scared of her. In her way she was kind to me as long as I worked and did everything I was told. I had to work more or less straight away - feeding the fowl and fetching the cows for milking, and I was the only one who could catch the horse. They had me as cheap labour, but I didn't complain. I still enjoy work now and I didn't want to go back to the children's home. That was always a threat if I didn't do as I was told.

My 'mother' worked hard, making butter, helping in the garden and with the cattle. She had a sit-up and beg bike and on one side she carried the butter, the other side the eggs and perhaps flowers on the back and she took them every Thursday to the sale at the Swan in Coleshill. You could live off a small holding then. My 'father' was very nice, but he had to buckle under 'mother.' He did all sort of jobs, as a gardener and a farm labourer when he was young. He worked at the vicarage and when he was learning to drive, he was reversing and said 'woa' as if he were a horse, and reversed into a tree!

I had a long walk across the fields to Maxstoke School. My 'father' said he used to go to Maxstoke School, riding a pig. Mrs. Haden was headmistress and Miss Edkins the infant teacher. We went in the field by the side of the school to play. I seemed to get on with the other children all right. We only had one math's book a year and when I finished mine, there wasn't another one to work through. I remember Daisy Baker had an argument with the teacher and she went off with the school keys and threw them in culvert. No one ever found them. I was only at Maxstoke School a year before I left to go to St. Pauls Central School in Coleshill. It was a Catholic School and you had the strap there, not the cane. I left school when I was fourteen.

Compiled from oral recording (1997)

Rosemarie Wall *(nee Beresford)*

My family moved from Derbyshire in 1935 and my father went to work for Mr. Antrobus at Hill Farm. I was born in 1936, the baby of the family, with three brothers and three sisters. We lived at Dukes Cottage, a small two up and two down - toilet across the garden and a tin bath by the fire on Friday nights. I started school in 1941, during the war and remember carrying a gas mask to school. A family of five evacuees and their dog 'Nigger' lived with us for two years, as their home had been bombed. They slept downstairs and we slept upstairs. It was very crammed. In winter, as soon as we got to school, the teacher made us a lovely hot drink of cocoa, and then we had prayers and a hymn. There were coke stoves in the classrooms and the school was divided in two by a wood and glass partition, which would be drawn back for the Christmas plays. There were about thirty-five children in school.

LESSONS IN THE PLAYGROUND

Mrs. Haden was a very strict head mistress. Miss Graveson, the infant teacher was lovely. On hot summer days, of which we had many, our class would go out in the playground for lessons and if we were very good, she would take us over the road to her father's farm for lessons on the lawn. On May Day we had great fun. We used to collect the May, (blossom off the hawthorn) find a stick we could hold and cover it in May and flowers. The old oak tree overhung the school playground and when I was nine, I tripped over its roots and broke my leg. Next, I was swinging on the back of a hay wagon and my brother was holding my legs. I fell and broke my arm in three places. We both became ill with scarlet fever and went to Catherine de Barnes isolation hospital. I remember itching under my plaster!

When I moved up to the 2nd class, Mrs. Bowden had recently become headmistress. She was very nice but would stand no nonsense. She had a cane standing up in the corner but I don't remember her using it. She taught me a lot, especially about embroidery and mental arithmetic. My three brothers and two sisters also attended Maxstoke School and we all have very happy memories.

SCHOOL CLOSURE

My own daughters were two of the last children to attend. There were about twenty-three children in the school with falling numbers. I felt very torn about closing the school but my husband disagreed with me, saying it would be better for the school to close as our children would do a lot better at a larger school with a broader curriculum. There were a lot of discussions and meetings and I was sad to see the school close in 1967.

Compiled from oral recording (1996)

Maxstoke School (1960's) *Left - boy standing against wall - David Rollason, girl on top of frame - Sandra Wall, girl swinging from centre - Heather Jones, girl stepping onto frame far right - Helen Purdy.*

CHAPTER EIGHT

Meriden School (1910-1920)

MERIDEN SCHOOL

Meriden is situated in the centre of England, on the old London to Holyhead Road and has always had a number of inns and hotels. Its ancient name was Alspath and belonged, in part, to Earl Leofric and Lady Godiva. It still retains some areas of ancient forest and an archery club. Extract from Kelly's Directory 1884: 'A society, called the Forest of Arden Archers, the Woodmen of Arden, was revived in 1783 and hold their meetings at Forest Hall, where also is deposited a horn, said to have been used by Robin Hood, who is traditionally stated to have competed here in olden times.'

CHARITY SCHOOLS

In 1841, there were 191 houses and 1071 inhabitants. Since then, the village has grown steadily and still has a good shopping centre, several hotels, inns, and a village green with a monument to cyclists. The Church of St. Lawrence was built on a hill, some distance from the main village below, and an early school may have been sited near the Church at 'Hill Orchard.' Meriden was fortunate to have charity schools, long before the state provided a free education. Henry Barnet, in 1781, left £500. in trust, to include provision for sending boys to school. The Right's

Land Charity in 1749, provided for teaching poor girls to read. Meriden also had the Union Work House and housed up to 130 destitute adults and children, from Meriden and eighteen surrounding parishes.

The Digby family lived at Meriden Hall and Kenelm Digby, in 1811, left two Coventry Canal Navigation shares in trust, to apply the dividends to support a charity school for female children under the patronage of his sister, Jane Mills. Land, called the Old Bowling Green, was leased from Lord Aylesford at 1s. a year for a schoolhouse to be built in 1813. In 1813, the dividend, from the two canal shares, was £80. per year. This paid for a mistress and for 24 girls to be clothed, usually when they left school. By 1833, the dividends had reduced to £64., and Jane Mills made up the deficit but clothing was discontinued and some girls paid to go to school.

Kenelm's brother, Wriothesley Digby, built a boys school about 1823, on land leased from Lord Aylesford. When he died, he left four shares to Meriden charities. Two of these shares were given to augment the existing boy's National School. Twelve boys were clothed and another twelve received hats and shoes. As the value of the shares diminished, the provision of clothing was discontinued.

NEW NATIONAL SCHOOL

A new National School for boys and girls was built in 1843, at the east end of the village, at a cost of £522. 3s 1d, raised by public subscription, with a house in the centre for the master and mistress. In 1850, John and Mrs. Nancy Kimpton were master and mistress. The school was well equipped compared to other village schools had had a library containing a collection of some 300 agricultural books, supported by the clergy, farmers and tradesmen. It had an excellent reputation as a good school and this was due, in part, to the selection of Mr. John Penrice, Head Teacher from 1903 - 1939. Below are extracts from two letters from a series of correspondence sent in 1903, to Rev. C.R. Digby, School Manager. (Originals at W.R.O. DR306/6.)

A new primary school on the Fillongley Road replaces the old building. Senior children are 'bussed' to the Heart of England School, Balsall Common. The old school is now used as a doctor's surgery.

'Centre' of England, Meriden (1910c)

Worcester, Lichfield & Hereford Training College,
Saltley, Birmingham.
4th April 1903

My Dear Sir,

Penrice tells me that he is applying to you. I think he is very likely to suit well. But you will be able to judge by his credentials. He was a very satisfactory student. I believe him to be very trustworthy. He is a type of man who I shall think myself fortunate in securing, if I were in your place.

I understand one or two students wrote to you, but I don't think any would be prepared to undertake the responsibility of a house. If advised, I can tell you what opinion we have formed on any of them.

Yours very truly,
F.W. Burbridge. (Canon Burbridge)

18 Weatheroak Road, Sparkhill.
2nd April 1903

Dear Sir,

I beg to make application for the position of Headmaster in Meriden National Schools. I heard of the vacancy through the Rev. J.W. Burbridge. At present, I am head assistant at Christ Church National School, Sparkbrook, where I have been living since leaving Saltley College in 1900.

My results at the Certificate Exams were:
1899: Part 1 2nd class. Part 2 1st class
1900: Part 1 1st class Part 2 2nd class

I have the Archbishop's Certificate, being head of College Scripture list in 1899 and 2nd in 1900. During my apprenticeship I gained 1st classes every year in Scripture. I hold Certificates in Model, Freehand, Light & Shade, Science Sub 1, Blackboard and Physiography. I also hold the Elementary Teachers Certificate granted by the Birmingham Athletic Institute.

My class place on leaving Saltley was 2nd. I was a volunteer in the Corps at College and so have a good knowledge of military drill. I was apprenticed at Lord Windsor's National School, Tardebrigge, which is a country mixed school, very similar to Meriden. At present I am taking a Mixed Std. V and therefore have had a good experience in dealing with boys and girls. If necessary I will forward names of referees and also testimonials.

Should my application be entertained, I should like to see you and also have a look at the schools if you would kindly answer by return. I could ride over on Saturday morning.

At present, I am not married but as at present arranged, I shall be during the summer holidays.

Yours obediently,
John Penrice

SCHOOL MANAGER'S RECORDS

The first Managers of Meriden School were appointed under the Education Act of 1902. They were: C.W. Digby, Meriden Hall, Foundation Manager. Col. Monkton. J.H. Thompson, Malthouse Farm. Rev. C.R. Digby, Meriden Vicarage. E.L. Melly, County Council. John Kibbler, (Bulls Head) Parish Council. The extracts show the active work of the School Managers and evening use of the school.

Meriden Church (2003)
(right) Hill Orchard - an earlier school

EXTRACTS FROM THE SCHOOL MANAGER'S RECORDS

2/7/1903	Rev. Digby requested use of the schoolroom on Friday evenings for choir practice.
24/7/1903	Rev. Digby drew attention, that in the H.M. Inspectors Report, a third assistant teacher was requested. It was agreed to advertise with a salary of £50.-£55. per annum. It was requested that a local person be found if possible.
28/9/1903	A letter from Mr. John Penrice (Head Master) requesting work on the drains. He also requested the schoolroom to be used for Technical Classes. An application from Miss Violet Glover asking for an increase in salary (from £5. per annum to £8. per annum) was carried. Rev. Digby asked that the Infant's Room could be used for meetings of the 'Young Men's Social Club'. Granted.
2/l2/1903	Miss Nelly Standish unanimously selected as Assistant Teacher.
4/1/1904	School closed due to Whooping Cough epidemic.
27/1/1904	The Master complained about bad quality of school coal supplied by Mr. Milward.
Feb 1904	School closed - medical order. Epidemic of Measles and Chicken Pox.
13/5/1904	Insurance of School Building was raised. Present insurance of £800 (School Building), £150 (Furniture), £50 (Outbuildings). These amounts considered below actual value. Agreed to increase to £2000. Mr. Penrice having submitted a request for an increase in salary on behalf of himself and Miss Stamford, the Infant Mistress. The Mangers decided to postpone its consideration until after H.M. Inspectors Report on the school has been received.
13/7/1904	The salary of Mr. Penrice be raised, £115. Miss Stamford + £4. to £55.

Meriden School (c1920's)
Left - Mr. Penrice. Right - Mr. Jones. Back Row: 3rd from right: J. Skidmore. 2nd from right: L. Warmingham. 3rd Row: (?), J. Hodgkins, ? Butters, B. Taylor, (?), W. Bentley, (?), (?), J. Savage. 2nd Row: (?), E. Glover, (?), B. Morris, (?), N. Poole, I. Woodfield, B Southern, I. Woodward. Front Row: B. Griffin, B. Harvey, H. Higginson, (?), J. Wilcox, E. Schuabel, N. Freeman, ? Williams.

A BOY NAMED 'PARKER'

From January to July of 1906, a considerable amount of correspondence went backwards and forwards between the Chief Attendance Office of Warwickshire County Council and Mr. Penrice, concerning a boy named Samuel Parker, aged eleven. The family lived in the adjacent parish of Berkswell and Mr. Parker had come to the school and presented his son, Samuel, for admission. Mr. Penrice refused to accept him. He considered it was 'purely a case of capricious removal,' and as the boy had been held in detention at Berkswell School for bad language etc., he did not want to admit him.

The boy's father, insisted on his right, as children from Meriden were attending Berkswell School. The local attendance officer made several visits to the family home, to try and resolve the stalemate. Mr. Parker was determined to have his son admitted as other boys were continually beating Samuel, quarrelling and causing unpleasantness. After more than six month's negotiation, the Education Officer and School Attendance Office suggested to Mr. Penrice, that 'on moral grounds, these boys should be separated.' They suggested a trial period at Meriden, and Mr. Penrice finally agreed.

AN INTERVIEW WITH MR. PENRICE

Extracts from the COVENTRY STANDARD *11th November 1939*

Asked to give his views on modern education, he replied in quite an optimistic way, that he considered today's method of education to be quite good. He holds the view, quite strongly, that half the child's time should be spent in reading, writing and arithmetic, and that the other half should be spent in practical instruction. Himself, a very active man, he introduced gardening, bee keeping, poultry keeping, woodwork, cooking and science into the school curriculum. In his early days, he organised a very successful evening school. However, as time went by, he realised that Meriden was becoming an urban district, and the schoolwork had to be brought more into line with the requirements of the city.

Asked to say what his aims were in teaching the children, he said that he tried to teach children to be clean and straight forward and to respect and obey their parents. He said he had always tried to work especially hard for the backward children and had always tried to keep the school surrounds neat and beautiful with flowers.

Meriden School (1920c)
Miss Wall - teacher. Top Row: D. Cooper, (?), B. Munton, S. Rogus, J. Hemmings, B. Warmingham, V. Jenkins, (?), B. Kemp, B. Jakeman. Centre Row: M. Wemsley, C. Nicholas, A. Farley, (?), A. Warman, W. Hollis, B. Tranter, W. Gist, N. Hammons. Front Row: (?), V. Tenage, M. Freeman, F. Higginson, F. Higton, M. Cresswell, ? Parker, N. Shirley, E. Midwinter.

History of Meriden School

Basil Warmingham

My grandfather, Edward Warmingham, ran the post office in Meriden in 1882. My father went to Meriden School and when he left school, he was packed off to London to work as a 'page boy' at the Ismian Gentleman's Club in Piccadilly. He lived in London for 18 years and met my mother who worked at the St. James Club. They returned to Meriden in 1911, when I was six months old. They had me and four more boys.

My father went to work for Triumph Motor Cycles and my aunt had the newsagents. My grandfather delivered the daily papers and my father delivered the Coventry Evening Telegraph. I had to help when I was older. I started school when I was four years old in 1915. Mr. Penrice was the Head teacher. Miss Wall, Mrs. Order and Mrs. Jenkins were teachers. Mr. Penrice was keen on gardening and two years running we won the school shield for the best-kept garden in Warwickshire. He was particular about the school gardens looking tidy and we were not allowed to set foot on the lawns. The playground was divided across the middle. The front part for the infants, older boys near the road and there were two horse chestnut trees that blew down in a gale. My younger brother helped plant two new trees in 1926.

The teachers were all right if you behaved yourself. If you misbehaved, you got the cane, but I never got it. The teachers used to say about me, that 'this is the boy who

Edward Warmingham

looks as though he had been in the dolly tub before school'. Sometimes the head would ask who had got a clean handkerchief, and if you had one, you were allowed home half an hour early. We had to salute the head master, vicar, or any of the nobility in the village and say 'good morning sir'. Every Empire Day, we had to parade and salute the flags. The vicar came twice a week to take scripture. At the end of term, he set up an examination paper and a prize for the best paper. I was school monitor and I had to set the blackboards up every morning. I also had to mow the lawns every Friday evening after school, unless it was wet, and then I had to comeback to do it on Saturday morning. In the holidays, we used to go potato and pea picking.

The school was extended before I left by another two classrooms as the numbers of children attending had grown. We played football, and cricket. The attendance officer, Mr. Fell, used to come quite often and if anyone wasn't going to school, he would see the parents. The caretakers were Mr. and Mrs. Hopkins and the toilets were old fashioned, outside buckets.

It was a good school and we had a good education. My brother passed to go to the Grammar School at Coleshill and he has been awarded an MBE for services to export. I left school when I was 14 years old. I went to work in the Repair Shop at Rudge Whitworth Cycles, in Spon End then to the Standard Motor Company.

Meriden children (c1923)
Back Row: W. Hollis, W. Gyist, C. Nicholls, B. Warmingham, L. Rogers, T. Farley, S. Rogers, B. Hodgkins, C. Jefcote, C. Hodgkins. Front Row: D. Higton, D. Rench, W. Carter, N. Freeman, G. Mills, C. Rogers, T. Carter, E. Hodgkins, J. Savage, M. Savage, A Bedhale, ? Weston, W. Shirley, A. Farley, C. Warmingham.

Compiled from oral recording (1990). Most of the Meriden photo were copied from Basil Warmingham's album. Copies of which may now be found in Warwick Record Office.

Meriden School, Empire Day (1920c)
Front row: 2nd left: Margaret Lindley. Back Row: 1st left with white hair ribbon - Emmy Jakeman.
Boy in uniform and hat - Basil Warmingham. Girl with garland of flowers in hair - Joan Penrice.
Britain - Hilda Wheatley. Back row: 5th from right - Madge Penrice. 4th - Ruth Thomson with
white bonnet. 2nd - Nellie Shirley with white bonnet.

Percy Leonard Tuckey

My father was the village butcher and a farmer. I was born in 1922 and I started school when I was five years old. I remember my first day; they had to take me on the carrier's bike because I didn't want to go. My teacher was Miss Hickton who was very nice but I kept trying to escape until I got used to it.

1895c) Left standing: Miss Higton. Back row: 3rd - H Edginton.
?nd - Doug Warmingham. Sitting Miss Terry. 1st boy left centre row
A. Barnett.

Mrs. Jenkins was nice but very strict and she had a little cane. She used to get a bit annoyed with one boy named Brown, who wasn't very good at schoolwork. One day, when she asked him to hold out his hand, he grabbed the cane and broke it in half. They let him leave school before he was fourteen. Children came to school from all around, there were paths to the school from across the fields. In the classrooms were coke stoves, and the caretaker came every morning to see to the fires. Quite a lot of lads passed and went to the Coleshill Grammar School. I didn't go as I was occupied with the family business and I didn't do any homework. It was a good school. The teachers were always helpful. The playground was divided into boys and girls sections although we were taught together. We had a school garden. I shared a plot of garden with another boy and we had the lawn to cut. I remember there used to be another small school near the church. It is called Hill Orchard now and a private house. I seem to remember handicapped children going there.

Compiled from interview.

Trixie (Beatrice) Postings (nee Dolphin)

I left Packington in 1923 when eleven. We had moved to the borders of Meriden and Allesley. I went to Meriden School and Mr Penrice was headmaster and I was friendly with his daughter, Joan. When I went to tea in the schoolhouse, I was allowed to walk on the lawns, which was a great privilege as none of the other children from school were allowed to. We had green school uniform, which I thought was marvelous.

They started cookery lessons and we wore stiff white starched aprons and cuffs and we also learnt to play hockey. One of the teachers was Mrs. Jenkins and she would give you the cane. We led her a dance. We put twigs in her bicycle spokes and would try to get her 'rattled' in the sewing class by constantly asking each other to 'pass the scissors, please.' The education at Meriden was very good but I wish I had been born now. Young people today have wonderful opportunities and I would have loved to have gone to university.

(1924c) Top: Dorothy Freeman, (?). Seated: (?), Joan Penrice, Trixie Dolphin, Laura Ravenhall

Compiled from oral recording (1996)
Further extract in Maxstoke Chapter.

John Wall

When Little Packington School closed in 1955, I went to Meriden School. I was seven years old and I was frightened to death. It seemed such a big school. My parents wouldn't let me go on my old bike so I had to walk. If you lived three miles or more away from school there was a scheme where you got a bike. Our cottage was just within the three miles, so I qualified for a pair of Wellington boots! It broke my heart because I didn't have a bike.

Meriden was a very good school. Discipline was harder and I remember getting into a lot of trouble. Mr. George Havercroft was head and all he had to do to come to school, was open his living room door! I enjoyed it there. When I was eleven, I went to Balsall Common, Heart of England School. It was another very good school. I had to walk almost three miles from Packington to Meriden and then catch a bus. I left school at fourteen and have been working ever since.

Compiled from oral recording (1996)
Further extract in Little Packington Chapter.

A newer school replaces the Victorian building
The old school has a new life as a doctor's surgery.

Maureen Baxter *(nee Haycox)*

OVER WHITACRE SCHOOL

I was born at Market Drayton and in 1935, we moved to Quarry Cottage, Over Whitacre. I went to Over Whitacre School when I was five. It was near the Church and very small with only two classrooms. Miss Oldham was the head mistress. When she left, Mrs. Ansty came. She used to hit us. My dad went up in the end and sorted her out! I got the cane for throwing a snowball and hitting someone in the face. It was an accident but I still got the cane. The education was very poor but I did learn to read and write.

SHUSTOKE VILLAGE SCHOOL

We moved to Shawbury when I was ten and I went to the old school at the back of the almshouses, by the Church. Dad bought two old bikes and he did them up so my sister and I could cycle. It was a long way and I was a bit frightened to go to school at first. Mrs Whitehead was the head and Mrs Allan her assistant. The education was better and I learnt how to knit and to do embroidery and all sorts.

Shustoke Church and Church Farm

We did history but we didn't do much geography and my arithmetic was dreadful! We went for nature walks and we played in the field by the Church on nice days. I won a school prize for poetry and I still write poetry today and now have eleven poems published. The toilets were buckets outside and very smelly. The school dentist used to come in his mobile van and I had lots of teeth taken out. The 'nit' nurse came and looked through our hair and at our hands to make sure they were clean. If you were away from

school, the truant officer came to see where you were. Some boys were a bit undisciplined and high-spirited, mostly farmer's sons and they used to get the cane. The school seemed overcrowded and we sat all close together. Mrs. Whitehead was strict but very kind. In October, we had a week off school for potato picking. Shustoke School was a very happy school. I left to go to Manor Park School in Nuneaton. We used to cycle to Arley Station and then catch a train.

SHAWBURY INDUSTRIAL SCHOOL

My dad was away through the war (1939 – 45) and when he came back, he had no work. When he saw a job advertised in the paper at Shawbury School, he applied for it and got it. We lived in one of the old cottages by the school, then we moved to a newly built house up the drive. I had a wonderful childhood there. My father was an Engineer and taught engineering and my mother became a Housemother. I was told not to talk to the Shawbury boys, but I used to. I felt sorry for them and I got into terrible trouble. Some boys were in for quite serious offences. They were such nice looking boys and as a teenager, I was a bit of a tearaway. My parents would make me stay in for several days if they found me talking to them.

We used to get our milk, vegetables and flowers from Mr. and Mrs Jones at Dandy's farm. The boys worked on the farm and in the gardens and supplied all the master's houses and the school. They were very strict with the boys. If a boy wouldn't get out of bed, my Dad would tip the bed up with the boy in it. They needed discipline and sometimes got the cane. Some boys ran away and my Dad had to go after them. They would hide in the woods but they never seemed to get very far. He took their belts off and tied their shoelaces together so that they couldn't run off while he brought them back.

The boys earned a little money for the work they did and on Friday night there was a tuck shop so that they could buy things. The school put on concerts and the boys acted and sang in them. Sometimes they put dances on.

Compiled from interview (1999)

CHAPTER NINE

Shawbury Industrial School (1980)

SHAWBURY INDUSTRIAL SCHOOL

Are children born equal or are some born bad? Why do some behave badly, steal or become violent? Complicated questions need complicated answers. Could we educate all children in responsible parenting? When a young person commits a crime, how do 'we,' as a society respond? Is it possible to give a teenager, with no hope, new confidence and train them for a future? This was what Shawbury School strived for.

Shawbury would seem an unlikely place to have a 'school' for criminal and delinquent boys. It is a small, secluded hamlet in the north of the parish of Fillongley, quite close to Shustoke and about nineteen miles from central Birmingham. It still retains a sense of the old forest of Arden, with narrow wooded lanes and pockets of ancient forest. The school was sometimes called Shustoke and sometimes Shawbury. It became the first 'certified' school funded by a municipal authority and remained in existence for more than one hundred years, successfully providing a training and refuge away from city life, for troubled youngsters.

Up to the middle of the 19th century, homeless or destitute children could be put in prison, the workhouse or given an apprenticeship and committed to long hours of labour. The industrial revolution and population explosion had forced families to move from the countryside, to find employment in towns and cities. Provision of good housing, sanitation and clean drinking water were dire and poverty forced very young children into terrible working conditions or stealing food to survive. Victorian writers brought to the public's attention desperate tales of such children with examples in Oliver Twist, the Little Match Girl and Tom in the Water Babies.

JUVENILE DELINQUENCY

In the 19th century, crime levels and juvenile delinquency were of serious concern to the Government, just as they are today. The Government appointed several Committees of Enquiry who reported on the terrible deprivations of children - but nothing was done, although a law was passed to reduce the working hours of children. Charities and individuals tried to help. John Pounds (1819) founded his Ragged Schools for the care of destitute children. The Philanthropic Society founded several schools and led the way in providing an education and training for boys who would otherwise be sent to prison. Many other people campaigned and worked towards improving standards for children. The Government passed the first 'Reformatory Schools Act' in 1854, which provided for juvenile offenders to go to one of these schools, instead of prison.

Aerial View,
Shawbury School

THE SHAWBERRIES

In 1868, Birmingham City Council leased and converted 'The Shawberries,' a Georgian country house with forty-five acres, into an Industrial School. On 28th March, the Labour Master, John Clarke, marched six boys from Shustoke Station to Shawbury. The first boy, (Number 1) was 'eleven year old redhead, son of a Birmingham Dissenter.' He was committed for five years. He left to join the army and later became a policeman. Number 2, was recorded as 'weak' and the register entry on November 1871 – 'dead'. Number 4, was 'habitually lazy, dirty and a thief.' On 1st April, he stole a book and umbrella from the visiting committee. On the 25th April, was accused of gambling. The reports on his progress over the next thirteen years, however, were all good.

Living conditions for staff and boys in the 19th century were poor. The house was never designed as a 'school' and the boys regime was severe, punitive and unloving but the provision of three meals a day, their own bed and daily education were an improvement to living on the streets or being imprisoned. The boys carried out most of the work, including the building works as part of their training. In 1874, the Council decided to purchase the house and added a new three-storied dormitory block and a dining room. The number of boys coming into care continued to increase, so in 1876, Dandy's Farm House next to the school with sixty acres were purchased for £4715. 00. By 1899, there were 156 boys in the School.

Mr. and Mrs. C.J. Vinall were the first master and matron. Many staff did not stay and the relationship deteriorated so much between staff and the Master, it led to a request from the School Committee, for the resignation of all staff.

Legend has it, that this was due to drunkenness among the staff. In 1886, the new master was Frederick Horth and the only staff to be re-appointed were Mr. Seal, Labour Master and Mr. Simpson, Master Tailor.

DANDY'S FARM

With the purchase of Dandy's Farm, boys could learn farming and supply the School with fresh food. Each department taught essential skills and provided the necessities for the boys and masters. The tailoring department made every boy a suit of clothes and the shoemaker's department kept all the boy's footwear in good repair. Other training included baking, laundry work, glazing, darning and whitewashing. The installation of the gas works for lighting with over sixty lamps brought another new trade.

WAYS TO SAVE MONEY

Although the school was almost self-sufficient, the cost to the Birmingham ratepayer was still high, at about £17.00 per boy per year. The Council looked for ways to save money and suitable boys were placed in apprenticeships, which for many children, was the worst form of legalised slave labour. Mr. J.T. Middlemore, (Town Councillor, School Committee member and later a Member of Parliament,) suggested that boys be sent to Canada and between 1884 - 9, fifty boys from Shawbury went, at a cost of only £10.00 per boy. A big saving to Birmingham City Council!

History of Shawbury School

FIRST 100 BOYS

Of the first 100 boys admitted to the school; 12 transferred to Catholic Schools, 5 to Reformatories, 4 died, 13 emigrated, 9 joined the Army, 4 the Navy, 11 became grooms or carters, 5 worked on farms, 31 followed various trades, 2 returned to the workhouse because of epilepsy and 2 were frequently in prison.

IMPROVING STANDARDS

Under the leadership of Mr. Horth, Shawbury became more liberal and a happier place. He was a keen cricketer and arranged matches between the School and other village teams. The School Band was popular and played at many of the local summer fetes. In 1897, the school was enlarged, with new dormitories, cottage accommodation for staff and a portable iron hospital with wards to isolate boys with contagious diseases. A schoolroom was provided instead of using the dormitories as classrooms. With water from a water tower, a plunge bath was installed.

Mr. Horth was the proud possessor of a Magic Lantern and the Vicar of Fillongley, Rev. Stevenson, enjoyed giving lectures. Between the two, they organised a series of lectures during the winter months in Fillongley and at Shawbury. This enabled the villagers to get to know and understand the lads better and to gain appreciation of the work done in an Industrial School.

The School became certified to accommodate 160 boys and London boys were sent to take up spare places. To save money, if the boy was of good character and had reached

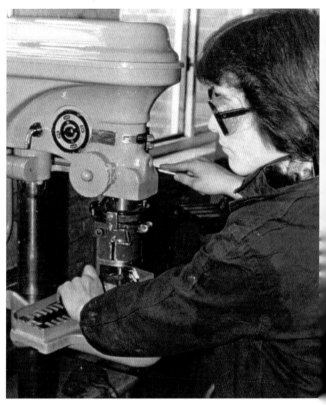

Engineering Training (1973c)

the age of fifteen, he could be released under license to any service, calling, trade or profession or helped to emigrate to a suitable job. The school was very successful and of 134 lads released between 1895 and 1897, 111 were doing well, 5 were doubtful, 6 unknown, 5 were dead and only 7 convicted of crime. When Mr. Horth left in July 1899, his progressive attitude had gained the school a good reputation. Mr. Craven-Jones commenced duties as the new head in September 1899.

CITY OF BIRMINGHAM
INDUSTRIAL SCHOOL SHUSTOKE
1906 Routine and Time Table

Monday – Friday

5.30 a.m.	Farm and Duty Boys Rise.
6.0 to 7.0 a.m.	Rise, Wash, Housework etc.
7.0 – 8.0 a.m.	Farm and Garden Work, Trades, Band Practice etc. 8.0 to 8.30 a.m. Breakfast
8.30 – 9.0 a.m.	Prayers, Religious Instruction, and Recreation.
9.0 – 12.20 a.m.	Sec. A. Secular Instruction (school). Sec. B. Farm and Trades
12.20 – 2 p.m.	Dinner and Recreation.
2.0 – 5.0 pm	Sec. A. Secular Instruction. Sec. B. Farm and Trades
5.0 – 6.30 p.m.	Wash, Recreation and Supper.
6.30 – 7.45 p.m.	Singing, Reading, Amusements, or Band Practice and drill.
7.45 – 8 p.m.	Prayers and Retire (Bathing: Friday Evening)

N.B. The section for Secular Instruction attends School on Alternate Days.

1914 – 1918 PREPARATION FOR WAR

With the onset of war, Shawbury was run on more military lines and boys were well grounded in military drill and the use of 'arms' as well as receiving an education and job training. Magistrates placed ever more boys into Shawbury, as they were concerned that the absence of the father, had removed effective parental control. Over three hundred and fifty Old Boys, answered the call to arms and Mr. Craven-Jones kept up a correspondence with a great number of them during the war. Of these, thirty-two gave their lives.

Improvements were regularly made to the School. The gas plant had been causing problems to the lighting, so by 1919, an electricity-generating plant had been made. Between 1924 and 1930, the heating apparatus was overhauled and the sewage disposal plant extended. The following letter is an unsolicited testimonial of school life at the time:

H.M. Borstal,
Portland,
July 1925.

Dear Sir,
This was my first visit to an Industrial School, and I was struck with the entire lack of the old useless discipline. I always understood that the discipline was hard and cruel, but it was pleasing to find it not so. I liked the absence of uniform too. The lads all looked cheerful and happy and I should imagine that the School is striving for the right method of dealing with young offenders. I only wish that I could have spent more time at the school.

Governor.

1924 - CHANGE OF NAME TO 'SHAWBURY SCHOOL'

It had been decided by the Home Office to discontinue the term 'Reformatory and Industrial Schools Department,' and to change it to 'Children's Branch'. Many schools changed their name during this period and 'Shustoke Industrial School' became 'Shawbury School'. The title of Superintendent was changed to that of Headmaster.

A Scout Troop was formed in 1929 using the old isolation hospital building as its headquarters. In 1931, after 32 years service, Mr. and Mrs. Craven-Jones retired. He had kept Shawbury in the forefront of all the Home Office schools. The new headmaster, Col. N.H. Mattock, had quite a challenge to change old methods. Boys under the age of fourteen were now required to spend more time in the schoolroom, and after that, spend half their time in one of the training departments. He arranged for a staff recreation and mess-room and a pleasant clubroom for senior boys. The annual seaside camp was discontinued in favour of smaller groups cycling to a weekend camp between Barford and Hampton Lucy.

FAILED EXPERIMENT ON SHORTER TRAINING

In 1935, Shawbury was one of two schools to run an experimental program to give boys aged between fourteen and seventeen, a much shorter training of between six and twelve months. With such a swiftly moving population, Staff could not provide in-depth training or have time to adequately cope with individual problems. The experiment failed and the School returned to the tried and tested program of a project approach to work. (The short, sharp, shock was to be tried again some fifty years later!)

PETS CORNER

The boys in the manual room constructed a pet's corner and in late 1936, lads had the opportunity to keep a small pet. It was an immediate success and within two months, they had pigeons, rabbits, mice, a tortoise, lovebirds, goldfish and even a bantam cock.

1938 - RUMBLINGS OF WAR

During the war, the School was run on quasi-military lines, and much made of drills and parades. In 1938, the boys worked through the winter preparing defences against air attack by digging a network of trenches and bunkers. In 1939, major works to the school commenced which included the demolition of an unsatisfactory wing. When living conditions could not have been worse, boys from the Remand Home at Moseley Road were evacuated to Shawbury. None of the new buildings were finished and some buildings completely demolished. All home leave was suspended. Four members of Staff left to join the Forces and the school struggled with only one resident male officer.

The first colony of bees was introduced in 1941 and after the fine summer, many of the senior boys went to help local farmers with harvesting and threshing. Shustoke Flight formed part of the Air Training Corps and by the end of the war, four hundred and eighty nine Old Boys had served their Country of which fifteen were killed.

(J.R. Jones. A.D. Quinn. S.W. Sutton. F.A. Vaughan. T.H. Quinney. H.R. Keen. J.T. Glover. D.J. Sharpe. A. Hardie. R. Carpenter. C. Bolton. T.M. Dutch. K. Downing. C.R. Smallman. R. Hall.)

After the war, there was a move against institutional regimentation. The School adopted a 'House' system. Tudor, Windsor, Westminster and Blenheim. The band died a natural death as the instruments wore out. In 1953, Col. and Mrs. Mattock retired and Mr. S.J. Hammond was appointed Head and his wife, Matron.

Shawbury boys made a special display stand for the old Fillongley School Bell (1970's)

1956 - SMOKING AND FIRES

A serious fire was discovered in the Gymnasium 7th July 1956 and the gym and store were gutted. Many instances of fire-raising occurred around this time and they coincided with the introduction of a smoking privilege for boys who were over 16 years of age and had their parent's consent.

The School continued to have improvements and the boys in the various departments carried out most of the work. The Headmaster's house, completed in 1964, was a joint project undertaken by the six major trade departments, built entirely by the boys except for the electrical wiring.

In 1960, on the retirement of Mr. Jones and Mr. Middlemiss, there was a complete re-organisation of the farm. Fruit trees were uprooted and a new Horticultural Block took five years to complete. The farm buildings were rebuilt and a yard and parlour system of milking introduced with a larger herd of cows. By 1967, eight breeding and fourteen fattening pens were nearing completion in the piggery for eight sows and one hundred and forty piglets. Boys could now learn horticulture as well as farming and other trades.

SCHOOL MAGAZINE AND GO KART-KLUB

For several years there was an annual School magazine, edited by Ian Glen. In 1967, the magazine gave details of various activities, academic results and sporting details. These were numerous and included football, cricket, rugby, basketball, athletics, weight lifting, annual cadet camp, trekking, chess, music club, farming club etc. Boys contributed with poems, short stories and their views. Reported in the magazine were the antics of a new 'Go Kart Klub' started by Windsor House, in a beg- borrowed sort of way with a 'Tro-Kart' powered by a 98cc chain-saw engine with petrol, siphoned from Mr. Glen's car. Needless to say it was not without a lot of problems and much fun. The kart engine conked out and was replaced with a 198cc Villiers 8E engine minus the gearbox. The new engine improved performance.

Extract…

> *'We soon found out who were the daredevil drivers. Keith Davis fancied himself as the Champion (idiot?) and one fine day decided to give us a demonstration of the wall-of-death ride. His super skill took him halfway up the tree in the middle of the field, and he was quietly removed from the Klub. About this time, a 250cc powered machine appeared on the scene, collided with the toilet wall, collapsed, and was quickly returned to the generous donor. At the moment, our own Kart is nearing completion in the engineers shop, built to our own design….'*

Go Kart-Klub (1967c)

THE TROUBLED 1970'S

The Headmaster, Mr. Hammond and his wife retired in 1970 and Mr. Brian Owen took over. In 1971/2, the school closed while major work and modernisation took place and Staff took the opportunity to retrain and get academic qualifications. The cost of modernisation was about £180,000. It was suggested at the time, the School should be bulldozed and that house units be constructed, but these ideas were dismissed as being too expensive. During the 1970's, coal was extracted from under Shawbury which caused subsidence. Another £250,000 was needed to rectify the problem, although the Coal Board should have financed this.

SOCIAL SERVICES DOSSIER

Shawbury had to continually keep changing and improving, in line with the prevailing Government dictum. In its latter years, the School had become part of the Birmingham Social Services Department and with the advent of the 'Social Worker,' another complication was introduced into rehabilitating young offenders. Staff felt that social workers mainly had theory, but not a practical approach to rehabilitation. Each boy had their own Social Worker who had a dossier on their behaviour and crimes. Shawbury staff did not see the dossier and each boy started with a clean slate. This meant that all boys were equal and none could be accused of former crimes. Form filling was kept to a minimum and the School liaised with the social worker, arranging home visits and rehabilitation etc.

The concept of training boys for a future was however, becoming old fashioned. Traditional values and practical experience remained at Shawbury and each boy, after an induction period, could choose which trade they would like to learn. These included engineering, woodwork, farming, horticulture, painting and decorating etc. Various activities, educational visits and camping expeditions broadened the boy's outlook. The boys became a trusted part of a small and close-knit community.

INCREASING JUVENILE CRIME RATES

In 1969, 818 boys were sent to borstal and 2228 were sent to a detention centre. By 1978, there was a massive increase with 2117 sent to borstal and 6303 sent to a detention centre. The success rate of detention centres was 27% and of borstals, 15%. Most boys went on to commit more crimes! The success rate at Shawbury in 1970 was about 70%. After this date, and no one was quite sure why, the government statistics show their success rate reduced to 50%, still much higher than any other institution?

In 1980, Shawbury had 66 places for young offenders but it was being sidelined and was only about two thirds full. The estimated cost of placing a young person in a borstal or similar institution, worked out at about £200.00 per week. At Shawbury, the estimated cost was £147.00 per pupil. Boys sent to Shawbury were financed by Social Services and Birmingham City Council. Boys sent to borstal were funded by Central Government.

SHOCK CLOSURE
AND POLITICAL DOGMA

Rumours circulated for some time, but it came as a shock in February 1980, when Staff were informed of the intention to close the school that summer and were given just one week to discuss and make comments. Ironically, the decision was made by the Tory run council who were 'tough on crime.' It was opposed by the Labour group, who, when they regained control a little later, did not rescind the closure. A big campaign was organised with petitions and appeals. In the 19th century, to save ratepayers money, boys were sent to Canada or as apprentices. In 1980, the way to save money was simply to close the school.

The Staff who were dedicated to their work, felt angry and powerless. The aftermath rippled on and many had the increased worry of not only losing their job but also their tied home. The Tory Council said that they would have the right to buy as a sitting tenant, but when Labour regained control, it scrapped the policy. Added to this, mining meant six of the twenty houses had suffered subsidence. The sewerage system was erratic and Severn Trent wanted £110,000 to maintain and modernise it. Birmingham Housing Department refused to take on the responsibility.

The City of Birmingham Estates Department put the school up for sale with tenders to be in by 8th August 1980. Dandy's Farm was sold but Shawbury became derelict and worthless. Several years later, it was sold to a property developer and the school demolished and attractive new homes built.

The staff houses remain and some former members of staff still live in them. 'Old boys' often return to Shawbury and are seen re-visiting their old haunts.

Most of this chapter has been compiled from a booklet researched by Ian Glen who taught at Shawbury School. A copy of this booklet has been placed at Warwick Record Office.

Staff (1978-80c)
Left to right: Back row: Ray Letts - Clerk, Peter Griffin - Paint/decorator, Mick Jerrard-Dinn - Asst. Farm Bailiff, John Cooper - Farm, John Graves - Teacher, Ian Whittaker - Carpenter, Roy Barrett - Engineer, Larry Meakin - Asst. Carpenter, Geoff Croft - Horticulture, Cameron Jones - Housemaster, Derek King - House Master. Centre Row: Ann Whitmore, Derek Lee - Bailiff, Mrs. P. ?, Frank Moody - House Master, Sid Wheele, Sheila Wheele, Len Warden - Teacher, Marlene Martin, Sheila Wade - Domestic, (?), Bernard Deeley - Storekeeper, Bert Webb - Building, Brian Tregawny - Maintenance. Front Row: Barbara Barrett - Domestic, Pat Griffin - Domestic, Mary Knowles - Asst. Matron, Mary Martin - Secretary, Roy Duffin - Builder, Brian Owen - Head, Derek Knowles - Dept. Head, Wyne Airdrie - Matron, Lucy Deeley - Cook, (?).

Roy Barrett

I was born in 1929 and went to school in Coventry. I did an Engineering apprenticeship at Lea Francis Cars and in 1970, I went into partnership, as a design consultant. We moved to Fillongley in 1963 and I was involved with the youth club as youth leader, for twelve years. It started by me kicking a ball around, and five of us ended up as one hundred and five!

Roy Barrett with engineering boys (1970c)

ENGINEERING INSTRUCTOR

We used to take members of the Youth Club to Shawbury to be entertained by the staff and boys.

They had first class equipment and we were able to use their facilities. We had nothing in the village for our boys, and they liked us mixing with them. After many visits, Brian Owen who was Head, invited me to have a look round and he took me into the engineering workshop. It was wonderful! Brian told me that it had been empty for twelve months as they had been unable to get an engineer to run it. I said, 'I'm an engineer,' and he said, 'You're just the man we need as an instructor.'

I went for teacher training to Huddersfield Polytechnic and stayed at Shawbury School until it closed in 1980. I had the freedom to teach my subject the way it seemed right. I wasn't tied down by examinations and curriculum. I could plan lessons to use each boy's natural talents, rather than force things upon them. When the boys first came, they had an induction for six weeks and then they could choose the department they wished to train in. Once they made their choice, they could not change. The boys were aged between fourteen and eighteen. To start with, they were often very aggressive, disruptive and anti-authority. They were separated from their family and they had been through the courts. They had probably committed many crimes before they came to us. They had lost their freedom and confidence and could be violent. As staff, we recognised this.

LASTING RELATIONSHIPS

Because it was a residential school, we built up lasting relationships with the boys. We got them up in the morning and played games with them in the evening. I had kids say to me, that I was more like a father than their own father, or that I was the first man who had ever said 'no' to them. I was sometimes the first person to attempt discipline and after a while, they recognised the discipline and that we cared for them.

The boys were never sentenced to a period of time. Each pupil had a monthly review, attended by himself, parents, social worker, internal social staff, teachers, and chaired by the Head. We reviewed the pupil's progress, behaviour and relationship with parents. In simple terms, if the Head Teacher could give three or four very good reviews, the boy could be released to wherever the social worker said he could go to.

TEACH THE PARENTS

If the lad had poor reviews, was lazy, disruptive or the parents were not prepared to have him back, he could be with us for two years. Some parents were all right, but some staff would say that we could help more, if we could have the parents at the school instead of the boys! When boys ran away, there was usually a reason. Often the outside social workers did not keep us informed of the problems. One boy kept running home and eventually we discovered the reason. His father was a drunk and his mother a prostitute. When he wasn't there, his mother went on the streets, but when he was there, she stayed at home with him.

TRAINING FOR WORK

We offered training to prepare the lads for work in either decorating, gardening, farming, carpentry, engineering or building and they were not allowed to leave until they had a job to go to. They also attended the school for a formal education in the afternoon. In the evening we organised activities and played games. We also arranged many outings. Sunday afternoon, parents visited, but it seemed that only the 'better' parents came. Many boys came from broken homes. When they left, they were different. They were disciplined and had a skill and confidence.

SCHOOL CLOSURE

For months, there were rumours, that the school was going to change or close. It made the staff very jittery. Finally, Edwina Curry, Head of Social Services came and held a staff meeting. We kind of expected it and one or two staff had already got other jobs. The powers that be, that wanted to close the school, said that boys should be fostered in nice homes instead of being at Shawbury. They simply didn't understand. What family could have taken lads straight from court? We knew we were doing the right thing. The staff had a wonderful feeling when the lads would shake your hand and say, 'Thank you,' and we had tears in our eyes when they left. It was the best job I have ever had, and I think we would all go back tomorrow.

Compiled from oral recording (1996)

Roy Barrett with engineering boys (1975c)

Ray Letts

The School is about 120 years old, but the actual house where the school originally started is much older and dates back to the middle of the 17th century, as a gentleman's country house. The school itself saw many changes. They had units for farming, horticulture, building construction, engineering, painting and decorating, carpentry and joinery and also domestic skills. In the hundred years it had been going there had been other types of training. They had cobbling (repairing shoes and boots), furrowing and all related matters within the farming community. The boys, in the early years, were set to farming tasks, because it was self contained and it was very much the master and the labourer.

WE WERE LIKE PARENTS

I worked in the office doing administration, until it closed. I also stood in for any staff if they were away. The boys looked upon Shawbury, silly as it sounds, as their second home. The people they were working with, got to know them well and we were like parents, which I suppose in a way we were. We were trying to instil in them, honesty, hard work and going straight.

In the middle of the 1970's, Birmingham decided to change Shawbury from an Approved School to Community School. This was brought about by the Young Person's Act, whereby you had a mixed school of young offenders and non-offenders. There was a lot of 'argument' about this. The idea was that the good would make the bad better. It doesn't work! So the lads that had never been in trouble took up with the bad ones and the traditional way we had been following, did not work. The school was closed as an economy cut. Today it is costing a lot more to do the same kind of work in the community.

Compiled from oral recording (1990)

Charles Morgan

POVERTY

I was born in Florence Street, Birmingham in 1920. I was the eldest of ten children. My father was invalided out of the army with trench feet. We had no money and I would have to get some money from somewhere. When I was seven, I used to go down to the market and get empty cases and chop them up in the cellar and sell them as firewood. I would get six or nine pence and give it to my parents and that was all the money that came in. My father at that time couldn't walk. We were very poor and hungry. There were three years between each of the children. Bread was about two pence and I felt the responsibility of the family and didn't go to school. They put me on probation for twelve months. The School Board man used to come and wait for me to come into the house and tell me that if I didn't go to school, I would be sent away. My father was very hard and strong and he had had a long session in the war and he drank. If I came into the house at a certain time, he would lock me down the cellar. Every halfpenny he got hold of, he would spend it. My mother couldn't stop him drinking.

Charles Morgan, aged 12, with his father on his day release (1932)

DIDN'T WANT TO KNOW ABOUT SCHOOL

My mother took me to a school in Bow Street and she would send me along the corridor. If I looked back and she wasn't there, I would leave the school and go round the markets to get some food. I didn't want to know about school. I had got into such a way of getting a few pence from anywhere. When I stayed at school, I was given a dinner ticket to go to another School in Bristol Street. You had to be quick to get to Bristol Street because they closed the door at 12.30 and they wouldn't let you in, even if you kicked it with your foot. There was no food at home so I would go hungry.

STOLE FOOD

Three of us ran away from home. We went to Thorpe Street Barracks and got into the gun limbers and pulled the canvas sheets over us and slept there the night. When the gates opened about eight o'clock, we slid out. We went down to a coffee house near the Hippodrome Theatre and when it was full, we went in amongst them and pinched a cake or two and then went down the markets. When I got home, the probation officer was waiting and a motorcar drew up outside. He said I hadn't been to school and without any hesitation, I was taken to a remand home in Moseley for three days. I went to court and Mrs. Cadbury was on the bench and she was sending the kids away for anything, to borstals and places.

When I went to court, my parents were there and they just sat there and said nothing. They read out the charge that I had not been to school and I would have to go to a reformatory school. I was eight years old and I didn't cry. I was quite a hard little boy. The two boys I ran away with were also sent away. Robinson, to a training ship and the other boy to a reformatory school. They sent me to Shawbury. I didn't see my mother again until I was twelve. My father came twice with my aunt. The first time they wouldn't let him in. The next time he came with some sweets and they let him in for a few minutes, then he was gone.

RELIEF TO GO TO SHAWBURY

It was a relief to get away from all the trouble at home. It was a hard school but it was good. I was so unhappy at home and there was nothing in the house. No food, nothing, just jam jars. I used to get clothes and boots from the Daily Mail Charity. The police gave these out from Digbeth Station. Stockings and corduroy trousers that cut into the back of your legs.

I forgot my family when I went to Shawbury. My hair was cut and I was scrubbed and bathed. I was given a small shirt, shorts and shoes and pushed out into the yard and the other kids came up to find out why I was there. Some had pinched a loaf of bread or had been caught round the markets pinching because they were hungry. I hadn't been caught because I was a fast runner. I could go past a shop with baskets of fruit and he would see me and know what I was going to do, but before he could catch me, I was up the road with two or three apples. I was very quick. Anything I got extra, I took home and put on the table or up the yard on top of the lavatory syston where my mother knew to find them.

FISH BONE STUCK UP FOR ME

I made close friends at Shawbury with a fellow named Hanson. We used to call him 'Fish Bone'. The other boys would initiate you when you got there by giving you a clouting or hold you upside down in the latrine and flush the toilet, but Fish Bone stuck up for me, I was only a little kid. Colonel Mattocks was the new headmaster and he was a big strong man. He was the one that gave us the cane. We used to have to stand in lines and he used to inspect us. He would come behind us and wrap the top of your head with his knuckles and flatten you. It would give you a flipping headache. He taught us about discipline and how to get things done and to look after yourself and your kit.

FAMILY MURDER

I was allowed home only once, for one day, when I was twelve. We were not allowed home for Christmas or holidays. When I went up our street, I was dressed well and the others weren't. I felt I was the lucky one. I thought I was better than them. Even though I was at a reformatory school, I had learnt my lesson and I had changed. I didn't want to go into our house. There was newspaper on the table and jam jars to drink from and a big pot on the stove. It didn't look right compared to the cleanliness of the school. I went to see my aunt, Sarah Castle, who lived three doors down. She didn't want to let me in. When she did, she told me that there had been a fight down the bottom of the road with her brothers Lotte and Jim. They were going to kill my Dad but it came wrong and Lotte killed my uncle Jim. She told me that, and then she wouldn't speak to me at all. I was glad to get on a train and go back to Shawbury.

At Shawbury, we got up at six o'clock. We slept on what they called biscuits, like the army with a rubber sheet under your sheet and they would come and inspect your bed and if you had wet it, you were sent down below and put in a big bath of cold water and hosed with cold water. That was supposed to cure you. To wash, we had to go to the row of taps in the washhouse and stand by your number with your tooth mug. We could go out into the yard until breakfast at eight and have a game until nine. After that, we were detailed either for work or school. It was good and there was always food. We had hard long dark bread loaves and porridge. Sunday we had an apple or an orange. The dinners were good, meat, potatoes and cabbage. We had a kit inspection every Saturday at two. We had three boot brushes and if you were one short, you would be due for a good hiding. My number was 2156. I took this other fellers brush, 2056, and changed it to 2156. The boy was due to go out soon and he was a big chap. I got a worse beating off him that I did the master.

PUNISHMENT

They were just getting rid of the birch and I had the cane once. They didn't give it you during the day. They would get you out of bed and make you go to the office. Boswell, the shoemaker would bend you down and you had to put your head through his legs. You got four or five of them. You could tell when someone had had it as they would stand by the radiators trying to thaw out. One master used to punish you by tying you, with your tie, to the radiators if you were misbehaving and it was red hot. The manual teacher used to bend you over the bench and hit you with a steel ruler if you measured something wrong.

LEARNT HOW TO DO MOST THINGS

We were 'learnt' how to do most things. We used to plough Top Patch with two horses. It was a fair few acres. We had good gardens and we practically kept the school going on what we grew and we had our own individual gardens. There was a barn and about six of us would have to wash potatoes and put them through the potato peeler. We had a cricket pitch and we played against the other reformatories and won three cups. We had to do drill and we marched to Church at Fillongley and we marched to Coleshill Cameo Cinema. If anyone's parents visited and they got two pence or something, we went to a sweet shop called Bagleys. I didn't get any money but another boy would give me some.

MUTINY

When I was about thirteen, we had what was called a mutiny. About twenty boys met in the gymnasium and got the Indian Clubs and climbed over the wall, and away they went. I watched them but I didn't want to go. Within a couple of hours, they were all caught, apart from two. Next morning, one boy had got as far as Birmingham. They were sorry they had done it and lined up every day, for days, for the cane.

When Teddy Tongue and Arthur Billington left, they more or less went straight into the army and sent me photos. I was fifteen and a half when I left. I knew I was going to leave but I didn't want to. They took me to the bottom of the big tower, which you were never normally allowed into. I tried suits on and was given two suits, two pairs of shoes, shirts, ties and a suitcase.

GOING HOME

My father was a hawker on the market and my family had moved to a different address, to a maisonette in Stetchford. I didn't like it there. My father was still drinking. I had only been home a couple of weeks when all my kit had gone. He had either pawned or sold it. All I had was a pair of flannels and a shirt. Some nights he would fetch us out of bed if he had some food, fish and chips or something. One day, I was playing football with some pals behind the cinema and afterwards we had a bottle of pop. He thought I was getting into trouble but I wasn't. He was vicious. He would knock me from one side of the house to the other. He put these scissors down my back and cut me down my back and punched my face. I pushed him away. He was trying to kill me. I put the lock on the door. He was sixteen or seventeen stone. He got a flat iron and he smashed the door down to try and get me. I climbed through the window and ran down the path to a neighbours. He got to the door and threw the iron at me. He beat my Mum up and my other brothers and sisters. He never changed and I left home to join the army. Later, I made a career in greyhound breeding.

Compiled from oral recording (1998)

Photos from India from ex 'Shawbury' boys, Albert Billington and Teddy Tongue (1938)

Memories of Shawbury School

Walter Jennings

My mother was a cheerful woman but not very bright. She had her first baby before she married and as a punishment, her father made her live in the washhouse with no bedclothes, summer and winter. A neighbour used to put packets of food on the wall that she could reach and the only time she could enter the house, was when her father was out. My father was born in 1866 and he worked at the Regent Hotel as a stoker. My mother went to work there and she became pregnant by him and he married her just before the baby was due. It wasn't a happy marriage; he was forty years older than her and had been married before with a grown-up family. I was born in 1935 and I have an older brother and sister, and two younger brothers.

VIOLENCE AND MURDER

We lived in a rented house, one step up from the pavement, in Windsor Street, Leamington Spa. There was no glass in the bedroom windows and sometimes no frames and the cellars underneath were rat infested. We had gaslights and a cooker but no hot water and the outside lavatory had blocked drains most of the time. We had no garden but there was a pigeon loft with a storeroom underneath which was rat infested. My father won several trophies for his pigeons. He had been married before and his daughter, Kathleen, lived on the top two floors with her family. We lived downstairs but we shared one of the rooms with Kathleen and her family. When you went through this room to the kitchen, Uncle Alf, if he were drunk, would kick or punch you. He was a violent man. On his return from Dunkirk, he discovered that Kathleen had become pregnant by another man who lived down the street. He sought the man out and kicked him about in the alley and the man died. Alf got six months for manslaughter.

By the time I was thirteen, my father was in his 80's and bedridden. One day, Alf and he were arguing and Alf picked up a chair and ripped the leg off and started beating my father about the head. I ran to the table and picked up a carving knife to stab him. As soon as Alf saw me with the knife he ran out and I chased after him. I was scared but we didn't have much more trouble after that.

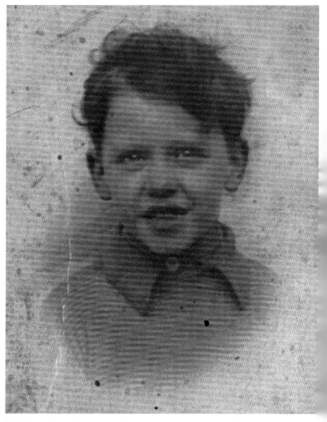

Walter Jennings, age 6

SEX BY THE PIANO

My father had a pension to support the family, but as each child began to work, the pension was cut accordingly, so you were in a poverty trap. My mother had been teetotal until a family tragedy led her to have a few drinks. She went to work as a barmaid and all her wages went on drink and she and Kathleen supplemented the pension by picking up men and there were occasions when she brought these men home. When I was eleven or twelve, I remember coming home and my mother was having sex with a man standing against the piano. I didn't realise what they were doing and the man kicked out at me and told me to F off. When my father became completely bedridden, he had no control over her, so she brought one man to live in the house. This was pretty common in the area. The neighbour next door was on the game and I saw one of her lodgers slash an American's penis because he wouldn't cough up the cash for services rendered. Many of the young people in the area had been to approved schools for one reason or the other.

I was regarded as a bookworm and was top in most subjects at school. I didn't have many friends and I wasn't a sociable sort of chap. My only good friend was David Thornhill. He was artistic and we would spend a lot of time in the countryside doing sketches. We had never any thought of getting into trouble. I wanted to go to the Grammar School, but my father refused permission as we couldn't afford the uniform and books. My headmaster, Mr. Harrison, came to see my father and tried to persuade him and said he would get all the necessary, but my father still refused to sign the papers. I was determined to go, so I forged my father's name. I passed the exam, but when it was found out, there was a rumpus and he still wouldn't let me go. I was devastated.

When I left school, I started work as an apprentice electrician and I had a lot of studying to do most nights. I kept friends with David and one day, we met a friend who was celebrating a christening. He had a bottle of wine, which we drank. We then met two other mates and they asked us if we wanted to go for a drive? Rowland O'Donnell said that he could borrow his brother's car so off we went. Someone had bought a bottle of cider, and we drank this as we were driving around. Unfortunately, they had stolen the car and the police stopped us near Warwick Castle.

INNOCENT BUT CONVICTED

Going to court and facing all this authority and having to cope with the fact that we were innocent, was pretty devastating. I was in a daze. Father was becoming senile and my mother didn't know how to respond or help. I felt I had been abandoned and there was no one to turn to. We were all charged with taking away a vehicle without the owners' consent and driving without a licence. I could not understand how I could be charged with this, when I was only a passenger? The two older boys admitted all kinds of crimes and David and I were tarnished with the same brush.

We were sent to Kings Norton Remand Home and Mr. Connelly, the Governor, called David and me into his office and said he thought that the magistrate was making an example of us, and that the court had been too heavy-handed. He wrote to the Home Secretary about it, but as no new evidence could be produced, we had to stay for assessment. David went to Banstead in Surrey and I went to Shawbury Industrial School, from February to November, 1952.

LOOKS A HARD CASE

Mr. Richards drove me to Shawbury. My first impression was of a magnificent, impressive building and I overheard someone say, 'My God, he looks like a hard case.' I had never been happy during my childhood and this showed in my face. I was introduced to various members of staff and I was to help Miss Jones, the Nursing Sister in the surgery. There were different occupations you could learn. The farm where you could learn to become a herdsman. The engineering shop, run by Mr. Cowell, (we called him Eggo because of his bald head) and he taught us workshop practices, sawing, operating the lathe and things that came in useful. We learnt maths, English and geography. I had never heard of Algebra until I went there. Mr. Doughty ran the Musical Appreciation classes and he introduced us to music and various forms of poetry. He was kind to me, except for once when he heard me swear. He marched me to the washhouses and washed my mouth out with soap.

I remember the dentist, Mr. Spooner, and before he had touched some boy's mouths, they were screaming with pain and terror! I mixed the fillings of mercury and cement powder with a pestle and mortar. Another of my duties was laying the tables in the dining room and clearing away. That included laying the table for the Colonel or whoever took his place on various occasions. This work put me in contact with the Chef and his assistant. The Chef had a fearsome appearance, tall with a twitch in his neck, but he had a heart of gold.

When I became more trusted, another of my duties was to escort people home of an evening. One person was a Scotch woman called Jean Urquart, a small slim lady with a harelip. She would put her arm through mine, and I was absolutely petrified. Miss Jones gave me little presents and once she gave me a small purse that had belonged to her grandmother. It had a small picture of Miss Jones in it and she said she hoped I would keep it and always look after it. I thought how wonderful that she should give me something that belonged to her Grandmother. I think that helped me to keep on the straight and narrow.

RUNNING THE TUCK SHOP

There were about one hundred boys in the school and they were divided into four houses. You started off as a beginner, then you became and improver, after that, you became a senior. There was a prefect for each house and then a senior prefect over the whole lot. You had a small amount of pocket money and this increased as you went along and there was a tuck shop where you could spend your earnings. There were boys in Shawbury who were willing to educate you into the things that you didn't want to know. I became a senior boy and then a prefect and it became my responsibility to run the tuck shop. One lad from Bristol helped me and was always saying, 'Come on, we'll get some Mars bars and we'll sell them on.' I said it was stupid as we weren't criminals and we mustn't steal.

ROLL YOUR OWN

When we walked to Fillongley, which was just over two miles, we would pick up any cigarette ends and take them back to make into cigarettes. We sometimes used pages from the bible to roll them in but they smoked all right. The dormitories had 15-20 beds in each and Mr. Halford, the Store Keeper, would come and switch the lights off. He had a saying 'All you who want to go to the latrines, go now, or forever hold your piece.' He would also go and tuck some of the boys in after lights out. The staff were all friendly and caring and made you feel part of a group. They took an interest in us as individuals although they never went into our case history. They made you feel you had a place in life and that you were important. It was a new experience for me to be in pleasant surroundings with clean sheets, blankets on my bed, clean laundry, clean underwear and have a toothbrush and toothpaste. At home, I had rubbed soot on my teeth to clean them, with my finger.

DECENT FOOTWEAR AND CLOTHING

The summer of 1952 was warm and sunny, so we spent a lot of time outside. For the first time, I had decent footwear and clothing. As a child, I would go to school in football boots or shoes that had cardboard covering a hole in the sole. Even to hear a radio was new as we didn't have one at home. I learnt about the world and the school had newspapers and a very good library. My mother and sister came to visit once and brought me a little food parcel. We didn't have anything to say to each other and so off they went.

During the summer I was allowed home for two weeks but I got the dates mixed up and a policeman came to the door to tell me to report back straight away. I ran out of the house, caught a bus, and three more busses later, I arrived at Fillongley. I ran the two miles to school and straight into Col. Mattocks study. He was sat at the table, and I collapsed to my knees. He told me to stand up and out of breath, I told him what had happened. I was frightened that I would have the book thrown at me. He was the most kindly man with a great sense of humour. He told me that he would look into it but I never heard anything more.

When I was home, Kathleen had asked me if I would like a cup of tea. All the cups were cracked and she was dirty with snuff stained mouth and nose. The gaslight hung over the table with a flypaper full of flies. As a fly fell in my tea, I realised how awful it was to be home in this ramshackle house after the cleanliness of school.

I gradually progressed to becoming Head Prefect. I was thrilled – it was an honour. At weekends, I could go out, walk down to the village and play sports. There was always something to do to keep fit and improve myself. The time at Shawbury went very quickly. I was happier there than I had ever been at home. I left Shawbury feeling that I had achieved something and Mr. Richards got me a job as an electrician's mate, with a local firm. I believe the proprietor of the firm had been in a similar situation to me, or someone in his family had. At eighteen, I was called up for National Service and I spent 5 years in the R.A.F. and trained to be an electrician. David Thornhill now lives in Coventry and from his skill as an artist, he set up his own little company engraving crystal and glassware.

Compiled from interview (1996)

Adrian Fraser

BABY DUMPED AT POLICE STATION

I was born in Halifax in 1959. My mother was Irish English and my father was Jamaican. I was born out of wedlock. My mother was already married so you can imagine what it was like when I arrived, a little half-caste. At six weeks old, my father and his sister took me away from my mother. So I was scuffed down Birmingham, living with my auntie, but my father didn't pay maintenance, so I was dumped at a police station at three months old. They put me into a children's home in Birmingham and I was fostered at eighteen months.

I remember as a kid, my foster Mum saying that they were not my real parents. I would ask, 'Why am I brown and why is my name Fraser and not Clarke?' It was war from day one. I always had a chip on my shoulder but the same foster parents cared for me all the way through. I was sent to an approved school in 1969 because the local school couldn't control me. The Council wrote to my foster parents, telling them not to contact me again and the council tried to get me to go back to my real father. I remember him walking down the yard, this big black man. I'd never seen black men as I'd been living in a little town. That's when I first met my brothers and sisters and I felt totally rejected. Six months later, the Council wrote to my foster parents and asked them to get in touch again because my behaviour got worse and worse.

Shawbury School Machine Shop

INSTITUTIONALISED

I went from one place to another and got thrown out each time. I was totally institutionalised and knew how to play the system but my foster parents still came to see me. Right up to 1981, I didn't care about them. It's only now I realise how good they were. I'd been thrown out of Forrell for fighting with the staff. The harder and bigger the reputation they had, the more of a challenge I had. All this you hear about 'pin down' or being 'molested,' there was never a problem and none of the approved schools did me any harm.

I ended up at Shawbury when I was sixteen. On the first day we went for a walk with Mr. Owen, the headmaster, and I pushed my luck so he gave me a right crack, a back-hander. It gave me respect.

It's hard to say how Shawbury reformed me. I went into the paint shop to start with and I had a lot of respect for Mr. Tregorren. He was a maintenance man and he was given boys to work with and he was very particular. I've always liked messing with cars and wagons and he got me going to work on a Saturday, at Skeltons in Fillongley, a tipper company. I was a dog's body, making tea and cleaning up. It was great.

SHAWBURY WAS DIFFERENT

Shawbury was different. Soon after I arrived, I had to go to court with my mates for stealing and petty thefts. Normally a lad goes to court with a prison officer or a member of staff. Mr. Owen came with me and he stuck up for me. He had got me then. I liked Shawbury; the staff had time for you. O.K., you got a clip round the ear. The best thing you can do with a thief is to put him in the situation of trust. Before I went to Shawbury, I thought I was the lowest of the low. One teacher at one of the schools said, 'You are not in here for winning Sunday school prizes!' We messed about and I got up to mischief, anything I could get away with! Mrs. Deeley was the cook, and she soon hit you with a ladle. She was centre-half with a heart of gold. Each member of staff had their own way. I remember Mr. Knowles getting us up at 4 a.m., and he made us run all round the lanes.

SENT TO PRISON

I stayed at Shawbury for twelve months. Even to this day, I call Mr. Owen, 'Dad.' If I have any hassle, I 'phone him up and he helps me out. When I left Shawbury, I worked in a fairground and I've been through that many jobs. In 1978, I got into trouble for stealing cars and trucks. I was nineteen and I went into detention and that was the last time. I did have a short spell in prison. I'd been made redundant and I'd bought a car with the money. I stripped it down in my bedroom, at my foster home. I went out and when I came back, my Mum had laid it all out in the garden. I can understand now why she did it, but at the time I went mad as it could have damaged the engine. My Mum had to call the police and I wrecked a police cell and fought with an officer, so they sent me to prison for criminal damage and fighting with an officer.

A BROTHER WITH SAME BEHAVIOUR PROBLEMS

I have a brother who has done very well. He went through exactly the same behaviour problems as me and we hadn't met then. I'm a skip driver now. Long hours, crap pay, but I love it. All my mates have come from broken homes but we've all succeeded. We're all tough. Inside myself, I've always been a happy person and I make the best of bad things.

Compiled from oral recording (1996)

Shawbury boys relaxing outside the school (1970's)

Robert Scattergood

I was born in Broad Lane, Fillongley, 1908. I remember the Industrial School when Craven Jones was in charge. There used to be a lot of boys there and 360 went to the First World War. They used to come from Birmingham, the naughty boys from Birmingham. Some boys were picked-up, off the streets. Old Johnny Boswell was one and Johnny Green and little Dicky Armsworth; they were all ex-Shawbury boys. They all had a good schooling there. What I used to like about Shawbury was that these lads had got a very good band, the bandmaster was Jones and one time, they had a drum and fife band. They used to come down to Fillongley Church, every Sunday. You know where the bridge is by the Cottage Inn, they used to assemble there and march to the Church gates and the band would be full blast all the way to Church. They used to go out to other places and into towns. I remember when one or two got away. One lad, they had to take to hospital as he had so many thorns in his feet. There was only one who got clean away and he was a gypsy. It was a very good school and it's a shame to see it now, all closed down. There used to be a lot of people on the service side, gardeners and those who worked on the farm and they used to teach the lads to do the farm work well.

Compiled from oral recording. Further extracts in book 'I Remember Strawberries & Sewage.'

ACKNOWLEDGEMENT

More than one hundred people have contributed to the making of this book and I would like to give my sincere thanks to everyone who has helped me. In particular, to those who shared their memories and allowed me to copy their photographs. To Roy Suddens, Mavis Hopkins, Jean Longfield, Clive Evrall, Nancy Bates, Janet Ryder and all members and friends of the Fillongley and Corley Local History Group. To Warwick Record Office for their help with research. To head teachers and staff at the various schools. To Paula and Roger Ball, Angela and David Currier and my husband, Lyndon, for checking text. Design by Lea Tatton of Garden Print. Without your help, this book could not have been produced.

Thank you

PHOTOGRAPHS

Most reproductions were copied from old photographs owned by contributors. Where the photographer or source is known, their name is acknowledged in the text. All recent photographs, (after 1980) were taken by the author. Many names of children and adults in the photographs have been forgotten in time. On the recent school photographs, names have not been included.

ILLUSTRATIONS

Children's drawings: (Attending Corley school 1995/6) FH - Fiona Heritage. NL - Niomi Luckett. AM - Amy Metcalf. LC - Lorna Crowley. JT - Jenny Thorogood. SN - Sam Nightingale. V - Victoria. GE - George Evans. (1985/9) CJM - Christopher Moore. All other pen and ink drawings, illustrations and page borders were by the author.

OTHER BOOKS

'I Remember Strawberries & Sewage'
A fascinating collection of twenty biographies, taken from oral recordings, which tell in simple words, life as it was, and as it is now. Price: £4.50 including postage and packaging.

'The Enchanted Castle'
An award winning children's book. The exciting story of two children who get lost in time. Christopher is captured by Lord Henry de Hastings and taken to Kenilworth Castle. His sister, Louise, has to find of way of rescuing him, with the help of Grumple Fairy and the Witch of Crackley Woods. Based on the history of Fillongley Castle and the siege at Kenilworth Castle in 1266. Price £8.50 including postage and packaging.

ABOUT THE AUTHOR

I was born in Huddersfield in 1948. My parents, Reg and Dorothy Calvert, converted an old bus to make their first home and travelled south. They tried various things to make a living and ended up in the entertainment business. When I was three, they bought a house but never settled and continued to move home every few years. After a disrupted education, I left school at the age of fifteen and attended evening classes, studying art, literature and history with the intention of going to Art College, to train as an art teacher. Life, however, has a way of not working out as you plan and instead, I got married, started my own business and now run 'Home From Home Accommodation U.K.' (www.homefromhomeaccom.co.uk)

With my family, we moved to Fillongley in 1980. Our daughter, Andrea, attended Herbert Fowler and our son, Christopher, went to Corley School. We enjoyed life in the village and with friends, started a history group. I began to record the memories of local people and copy their old photographs. I soon realised, I had captured something quite special and compiled my first book, 'I Remember Strawberries & Sewage.' At the same time, I discovered in the bordering parishes, some very unusual schools that ought to be researched.

A busy life bringing up my children, running a business, drawing and painting, and two more books, all helped to delay the publication of this book. I have always loved telling my children fairy stories, so when my son, who was aged eight, asked me to tell him a story about Fillongley Castle, I found myself researching, writing and illustrating 'The Enchanted Castle.' In the millennium year, with my camera, I helped to produce a book that recorded the life in Fillongley and Corley during the year of 2000.

It has taken some twenty years for this book to grow to fruition, but with each year it was delayed, more history, photographs and memories have been included. I have learnt so much and see history going in full circle. The same problems as one hundred years ago, torment governments and teachers as they continue to grapple with the thorny problem of funding schools and the best way to educate, unruly, 'free-range,' children!

TRANSPORT

"My parents moved to Colliers Oak in 1900 and I started at Fillongley School when I was five. My sister used to push me in a pram, about two miles. Some of the old folk used to say 'Make him get out and walk,' for she was only a little girl."

Ernest Gazey.

Within a radius of some four miles of Fillongley were eleven unique village schools. It is difficult to imagine how remote they were when the only public transport was a carrier's cart or steam train. Few children would travel far from their own locality and a trip to a neighbouring town or city would be a special treat. With the advent of the bicycle and omnibus, councils were able to close small schools and send pupils to larger village and town schools. Most church schools lacked resources and provided a very limited education that depended greatly on the personality of the head teacher.

With transport available, parents may select the school they consider most suitable for their child. Today, few children have the pleasure of walking to school across fields or down quiet country lanes.